MARKETING MASTERS

MARKETING MASTERS

lessons in the art of marketing
★ from those who do it best ★

PAUL B. BROWN

1817

HARPER & ROW, PUBLISHERS

NEW YORK, CAMBRIDGE, PHILADELPHIA

SAN FRANCISCO, WASHINGTON, LONDON, MEXICO CITY

SÃO PAULO, SINGAPORE, SYDNEY

FIRST EDITION

Designer: Ruth Bornschlegel

Copyeditor: Brian Hotchkiss

Indexer: Maro Riofrancos

Library of Congress Cataloging-in-Publication Data
Brown, Paul B.
  Marketing masters.
  Includes index.
  1. Marketing—United States—Case studies. 2. Success in business—United States—Case studies. I. Title.
HF5415.1.B79   1988   658.8   87-45601
ISBN 0-06-015868-9

---

88   89   90   91   92   RRD   10   9   8   7   6   5   4   3   2   1

As promised, this is for Peter James Peck Brown

Contents

1. What it takes to succeed today   1

2. The bull is back: Breaking through the clutter   12

3. We got the juice: The importance of being different   41

4. Zap! You're it!: How to build a successful product   75

5. "Hi ho Silver": Selling to a crowd of nonbuyers   106

6. The art of copying: "How to be a fast second"   137

7. Bricks, mortar, and pizza: Defining your resources   168

8. Conclusion: Tailfins will be back   202

Acknowledgments   209

Index   211

1 | What it takes to succeed today

A rising star at Booz Allen & Hamilton is munching on his shrimp and cashew nuts at the Chinese restaurant across the street from his Park Avenue office. It's been a tough week. He's put in three consecutive fourteen-hour days at the management consulting firm and there will be a six-hour plane trip tomorrow. Despite his $110,000 annual salary, the consultant feels unappreciated. He finishes his second beer and starts complaining about the firm in general, and about a senior partner he has been working with in particular.

"Right there, at the very beginning of the presentation to the client, he has a slide that says 'Nothing is constant but change,'" the consultant recalls in a tone that makes it clear he has *never* said anything that trite.

He stops and calls for another beer. "I am proud to say, I didn't write that."

The rising star's attitude is typical of hard-charging Harvard MBAs everywhere. And in making fun of the slide, the bright young man is right—in part. To say everything is always changing is true, but meaningless. It doesn't tell you how to anticipate change, or how to deal with it when it occurs.

But to completely dismiss the observation is to miss the point. Change *is* constant. And never has the business world been changing more rapidly. Here's just one graphic example: Every 58 minutes, a new product fails as a result of changes in the marketplace.

Those who master change succeed. Those who don't, fail. It is that simple.

Marketing Masters is a behind-the-scenes look at how America's best companies anticipate change and use new-found techniques to topple competition. You'll see how Pepsi developed a new soft drink and put the rest of the industry on the defensive. How Southwestern Bell discovered—almost before anyone else—what will be the "hot" market for the rest of the century, and how The Limited recognized before everyone else that department stores were becoming retailing's version of the dinosaur and designed a marketing strategy that would change the way women buy clothes.

The conclusions these companies reached and the tactics they used may surprise you. But that is to be expected, since change is quickly making everything you know about marketing obsolete. Just consider three companies that not too long ago were marketing stars:

•	*Procter & Gamble.* For decades, financial writers, Wall Street analysts and business professors used the company's name as a shorthand way of saying marketing powerhouse. From Crest to Pampers, the company was the marketing model. No longer. Thanks to increased competition in virtually every one of its markets, its steady growth is a thing of the past, both here and overseas, and the company is groping for new ways to compete.

•	*Philip Morris.* In the process of making the Marlboro man part of the American culture, the company created a phenomenal success. One out of every five packs of cigarettes sold now carries the Marlboro name. When PM went on to create Lite Beer from Miller, its place in the marketing heavens seemed assured. But now its star is falling. The most recent example is Seven-Up. PM spent $520 million to acquire Seven-Up in 1978 and proceeded to lose hundreds of millions of dollars trying to revive the soft drink. It couldn't. Philip Morris finally gave up. It dismantled Seven-Up and sold off the pieces—at a loss.

• *Kodak.* The company's name once was synonymous with photography. Once, but no longer. Arrogant enough to think that the Japanese could never match its quality or sales prowess, Kodak ignored the imports when they started nibbling at its market. Instead, it decided to battle Polaroid head-to-head in instant photography. It lost on both fronts. The Japanese now own the 35mm market —one that by all rights should have been Kodak's—and Polaroid's successful patent infringement suit forced Kodak to abandon instant photography. Today, instead of being a marketing star, Kodak's future is in doubt.

All of these giants stumbled because they could not adapt to a changing marketplace. They had forgotten, or had chosen to ignore, the very essence of marketing strategy.

Marketing made simple

When you strip away all the buzzwords, marketing is really pretty simple. You determine who you want to sell to and then you figure out how to get them to buy. That hasn't changed. But everything else has.

Until recently, if you understood the game, you won— even if you didn't play very well.

First, the pie kept getting bigger. The population was growing and the percentage of women in the workforce was growing even faster. In 1948, one out of every three women worked. By 1985, the majority of homes had two paychecks coming in and the results were dramatic. Sales of everything from frozen dinners to VCRs zoomed. When people have more money to spend, it is easy for marketers to look smart. Almost anything they do will lead to greater sales.

Second, the managers of marketing companies became used to working in an economy where inflation was the rule—and inflation makes your results look better than they really are. Even if unit sales aren't increasing, inflation allows you to keep raising prices. The company reports higher revenues, and it is easy to forget you really aren't growing.

An expanding market, coupled with the ability to raise prices virtually at will, meant that marketers faced little competition. My company could grow and yours could too. We didn't have to battle head-to-head. There was plenty for everybody.

Well, those days are gone. The days of explosive population growth are over, so you can no longer count on an increasing market to give you greater sales. Neither can you count on an ever-growing number of working women. Today, about six out of every ten women work, and that is expected to remain constant in coming years.

And what's even worse is there is more competition than ever before. Not only are you battling the company down the block, you are fighting firms from overseas as well. A few years ago, when we talked about international competition, what we discussed was the problems of selling *our* products overseas. Today, of course, those discussions are far different. As the Toyotas, Seikos and European designer clothing that you see every day show, the traffic has gone both ways for some time.

What this means is the days of easy growth are over. And without inflation, there is just no way to hide that fact.

We are now in a zero-sum game, where any increase in market share must come out of someone else's hide. If I win, you have to lose.

That, as economists are fond of saying, is the macro picture and most companies have become pretty good at mouthing the appropriate responses to the changing economic environment. You hear lots of talk about "managing in a period of disinflation," and how "we must run our company in such a way as to produce real growth." They lop off thousands of employees and shift labor-intensive work overseas.

All that is fine, but it misses a more subtle point. It is more than economic conditions that have changed. The people to whom companies are trying to sell have changed as well.

The biggest factor in the change is the baby-boomers. And by baby-boomers we are not talking the young urban professionals, who consider owning a BMW a divine right. These most-publicized of people are certainly baby-boomers, but there are not enough of them to make a difference. They represent, according to best estimates, about 4 percent of the total population.

It is not Yuppies who have changed marketing. It is the baby-boomers as a whole—that group of 76 million people born between 1946 and 1964. Demographers like to refer to this group as "the pig in the python," a large mass that distends everything in its path. The description, while macabre, is accurate. When you have a group this large—and they make up about a third of the population—it will change everything. And they have done that in the simplest way of all. They have grown up.

Back in the 1960s, a popular button read: "Don't trust anyone over 30." Now you have to. For the first time ever, most of the population is over 30. The median age is about 33. But not only is the country older, it is smarter. The percentage of college-educated people is higher than it has ever been.

Why does this matter? It's simple: Older, better-educated people become more selective. They don't necessarily want what everyone else has. If that is true—and it is—you must change your sales efforts. You can no longer hope for stellar results by aiming at the mass market. The mass market, as we will see, is splintering.

Here is a quick example. Look at the shelves when you go to the supermarket. You can now choose from a score of premium ice creams, in flavors ranging from cookies-and-cream to toffee, made by at least a dozen firms. Not that long ago, if you wanted ice cream, you were pretty much limited to vanilla, chocolate and strawberry, made by a handful of companies.

More significantly, you can see that splintering when you look at retail numbers.

It probably won't surprise you to hear that sales of specialty retailers—everyone from Toys-R-Us to The Limited—are growing far faster than department stores. What may come as a surprise is that their sales are now about equal. And the balance is clearly in favor of specialization. When was the last time you read about a traditional mass merchant—like Sears or Montgomery Ward—announcing it would open more department stores? They haven't in a long, long time. Instead, they open specialty stores or mini department stores, department stores that don't have a complete line of merchandise.

Sears and its progeny were classic department stores. But it doesn't do you much good to be a classic mass marketer when the mass market is fading. And clearly, mass merchants are fading fast. Department stores have been squeezed at the low-end by discounters such as Wal-Mart and at the high end by specialty shops.

And it is not just in retailing that you can document the decline of the middle market. Remember Howard Johnson? For more than 20 years the orange roof dominated restaurant marketing. To get an idea of its scope, consider this. In 1965 Howard Johnson's sales exceeded those of McDonald's, Burger King and Kentucky Fried Chicken—*combined!*

Howard Johnson was the place that fathers of all those baby-boomers would stop on the long ride to see Grandma or Mickey Mouse.

Today, Dad could stop at McDonald's, Wendy's or Burger King—and that is just at the low end of the market. If he has more time and money, he could pull into one of the scores of specialty restaurants that serve Mexican food, steak, seafood or whatever. Howard Johnson never really tried to adapt to the changing market. As a result, its empire was sold off in pieces.

Attention, K Mart millionaires

Okay, so the mass market is splintering. But why blame it on baby-boomers? Couldn't these changes be occurring because the middle class is disappearing, as some have suggested?

No, not really.

It is true that government statistics have shown for years that we are inching toward a nation of the lower-middle class and the upper-middle class. And that change is obviously important. But to look at just the economic data is to miss the point. The decline of the mass market is being caused by a change in attitude, more than anything else.

If the decline of the mass market was caused totally by economics, you could look at the statistics and say we are on our way to becoming a nation of upscale shoppers and downscale shoppers. Poor people will only buy inexpensive goods, and the rich will only shop on Rodeo Drive, the Miracle Mile and Madison Avenue. That process has already begun, you would say smugly. That's why mass merchants are in trouble.

But common sense tells you that's not what is going on. You see inner-city stores selling pints of Häagen Dazs ice cream, and you also see millionaires buying at K Mart. A shift in economics doesn't explain that. The real explanation goes back to the maturing of America.

As people become older and better educated, they are exposed to more. They try more things, and when they do, they discover there is more to life than buying a Chevrolet, shopping at Sears and stopping on the way home for a burger. They find they have more choices and they exercise them. That's why people with money often shop at discount stores and traditional downscale shoppers occasionally buy premium products.

Sure, some people still go to only one store to buy everything. But as the sales numbers at Montgomery Ward and Sears and J.C. Penney show, there are fewer of those people every day. That's the real reason the middle is shrinking.

Middle America is now composed of individuals who shop daily, and make decisions daily. Some days they go strictly for convenience. Look at the rise of Domino's Pizza, which guarantees delivery within 30 minutes, and all the chains like 7–Eleven. Other days they make decisions based solely on the question of price. And sometimes they trade off on the same shopping trip. The shopper who chooses one of those 20 premium ice creams may also pick a generic ketchup and a store-brand jar of pickles before he leaves the supermarket.

These attitudes—which weren't around when keeping up with the Joneses was an apt description of the way people bought—put far greater demands on marketers. They are making stars out of companies like The Limited, which combines a wide selection of just a few lines of apparel with excellent service, and are forcing others to change, or fade away.

Grown-ups are not going to pay huge mark-ups to traditional retailers such as department stores who provide services of dubious value. If customers—especially those who are members of two-income families who, by definition, have less time to shop—find stores that have little sales help and a limited selection, they'll go elsewhere. That's the real reason mass marketers are failing.

It is also the reason specialty shops and direct marketers are thriving.

The specialty shop is the inevitable result of the consumer's dissatisfaction with stores that carry the same products, display them in the same way and either have too few salespeople or too many who know too little.

A better-educated consumer who has been exposed to more through travel and the media simply will not put up with that kind of retailing. After waiting 20 minutes for someone to take his money at a department store, he'll decide that there has to be a better way. Once he does, the specialists have won. Consumers will go where there is a large selection of what they need. They'll choose to buy lingerie at a store that carries nothing but intimate apparel (e.g., Victoria's Secret) instead of buying underwear at the lingerie section of a department store. They may even choose to eliminate going to the store entirely by buying through a mail-order catalog.

The consumer has changed. And if marketers want to survive, they must change with them. Otherwise, they'll go the way of Howard Johnson.

Another quick example: In the 1960s, marketing gurus were saying the future looked bleak for Coke and Pepsi, while General Foods and other producers of coffee would continue to do well. Why? History showed that, as they grew older, people switched from soft drinks to coffee and tea.

But history did not repeat. The generation raised on sweet bubbly drinks stayed with them. Per capita consumption of coffee dropped 13.6 percent between 1976 and 1986, while people drank nearly 50 percent more soft drinks. Today people drink more soda pop than water.

The market changed. Pepsi, as we will see, understood that change, and introduced Slice, a soft drink with 10 percent fruit juice. The juice attracted the new health-conscious consumer and stole the fizz from Seven-Up's sales.

The best companies will realize that they can no longer draw a straight line from the past into the future. They will look around them and ask, where is this changing environment creating opportunity? That is what Southwestern Bell did with the Silver Pages, a telephone directory geared to older people. It understood that the nation is getting older. People over 50 now make up 25 percent of the population, and they are the fastest growing segment of the population. More important, they have a disproportionate share of the nation's wealth, *nearly half of the nation's disposable income.*

The elderly are a terrific market to be courting, and one that not many marketers have gone after.

That will change. Most marketers will soon realize they can't be in the middle any more, trying to offer the greatest number of goods to the greatest number of people. They are now selling to a new kind of customer, one who is smarter, has less time to shop and demands more. He is different from who he was in the past. Aging baby-boomers continue to drink soft drinks. Older people have more money. The market is changing.

To succeed, you must change with it.

The bull is back: Breaking through the clutter

The forty-sixth floor of the Merrill Lynch building in lower Manhattan radiates wealth and power—subtly. The beige carpeting is thick. The walls are burnished walnut. And the views are spectacular.

As you wait on the executive floor, you can stare out the seven-foot-tall windows and watch the boats ferrying tourists to the Statue of Liberty and follow the oil barges heading to the storage tanks on the Brooklyn docks beyond.

Entering the executive dining room, the image of wealth and power is only reinforced. Black leather banquettes, each with a fresh iris on the table, line the walls. The tuxedo-clad waiter places a sterling silver pot of coffee on top of the white linen cloth as you sit down; the Oneida sterling silverware—the Silversmith pattern, which retails for $55 a place setting—is suitably heavy.

But why didn't Merrill Lynch's corporate image match the surroundings? That was the question Jim Murphy asked himself shortly after arriving at the company's headquarters in the shadow of the World Trade Center. Merrill had hired balding, bespectacled James E. Murphy away from Beatrice Cos. in 1983 to oversee its corporate image. He would be in charge of everything from advertising and public relations to deciding what kind of

DAVID BELL of Bozell Jacobs Kenyon & Eckhardt

business cards its 115,000 employees would carry. And what Murphy found was an image in disarray.

Following a plan created by former chairman, Donald Regan, who went on to serve as President Reagan's chief of staff, Merrill had gone on a buying spree shortly before Murphy's arrival. It had acquired insurance and real estate firms and had also moved into investment banking to supplement its retail brokerage business. Supplying financial expertise to corporations now accounted for 40 percent of revenues.

These additions created the nation's largest financial institution—and an uncertain corporate image.

What exactly did Merrill Lynch stand for to the world beyond 165 Broadway in the heart of Manhattan's financial district? Each division had a different logo. Despite the push into other financial services, its 11,000 stockbrokers—now called account executives—still made most of their money selling stocks and bonds and saw little reason to change the way they had always done business. And if you received brochures from Merrill's real estate division, investment bankers or account executives, you'd be hard pressed to tell they came from the same firm. They didn't look alike or even present the same overall investment strategy. A consultant Murphy hired shortly after he arrived says: "Merrill Lynch's image was in absolute chaos."

In a service business that can be fatal. In all service businesses (and although they don't like to think this way, investment bankers, just like the people who flip hamburgers at McDonald's, are in the service business) image is vital. It is upon image and reputation that people pick one service company over another. Taking excellent care of a customer may help you keep a client, but you'll never get a chance to prove how good you are unless someone gives you a try. And people won't give you that chance unless they can figure out why you are better than your competition. In large part, you tell them why you are better through the image you project, and an "image . . . in absolute chaos" is not going to attract many people.

But bad as its images were, Merrill's advertising was even worse. It went beyond awful. You might at least *remember* a truly terrible ad. Merrill's advertising was invisible. That's no easy trick when you are spending $50 million a year trying to get your message across.

What made Murphy particularly uncomfortable as he reviewed Merrill's print ads and commercials was the memory of what had come before. In the 1970s, ads for Merrill Lynch were some of the best ever done. "Merrill Lynch, a breed apart" and "Merrill Lynch, bullish on America" had become a part of the American psyche. The Merrill Lynch bull, whether running along the beach or carefully wending its way through a china shop, had become one of the most recognized corporate symbols—and one that was absolutely perfect for the company.

"There are various images that come out of having the bull as your symbol," Murphy explains. "First, the bull is strong and positive. Then you have the bull [optimistic] and bear [pessimistic] language of Wall Street that plays into it. The bull was a made-in-heaven symbol for a company like Merrill Lynch." It was also a symbol that differentiated Merrill from its competitors. All investment banking firms may be more or less the same, but the bull positioned Merrill as being different. A breed apart.

The bull—or more precisely, a thundering herd of them—made its debut in the "Merrill Lynch is bullish on America" campaign Ogilvy & Mather created in 1971. And as a viewer watched those bulls thundering across an open range, or along a deserted beach at sunrise, there was no doubt that the bulls—and the investment firm they represented—were a power to be reckoned with.

"The campaign was brilliant and it brought together several things simultaneously," says Murphy, whose voice booms even when a listener is sitting less than two feet away. "It tied us to a bullish stock market. And also you'll remember the ads were running when there was a low ebb of patriotism. The line 'bullish on America' stood out.

"Everything had come together to create an almost indelible mark on the American public."

In 1986, private polls taken by Merrill Lynch showed that 60 percent of Americans could tell you that "Merrill Lynch is bullish on America," was the company's slogan. In advertising circles, where tag lines come and go every six months, that is remarkable.

There was just one thing wrong with the results of those surveys: Merrill Lynch hadn't used the bullish on America slogan in seven years—not since it had dropped Ogilvy & Mather.

Thinning out the herd

While there had been nothing wrong with the ad agency's work, O&M's management committed a cardinal sin: It insulted the client. In 1978 Ogilvy & Mather, the company that had created "The Man in the Hathaway Shirt" and ads for Rolls Royce ("At 60 miles an hour, the loudest noise in the new Rolls Royce comes from the electric clock") announced that it wanted to sell some of its stock to the public. Nothing unusual there, agencies do that all the time. But O&M announced it would use First Boston—not Merrill Lynch—as its underwriter.

A furious Don Regan fired O&M on the spot and put Merrill's advertising business up for grabs. After he cooled down, Regan allowed O&M to battle a handful of agencies for the right to retain the business it had had for more than seven years, but O&M lost the fight. Young & Rubicam would be Merrill's new agency.

In one of its first moves after taking over in 1979, Y&R reduced the thundering herd to one and created a new slogan: "Merrill Lynch, a breed apart." The ads (one showed the bull wandering successfully out of a maze which represented financial options; another put the bull in a china shop and showed it to be agile enough to maneuver around the porcelain without breaking a thing) continued to win the respect of viewers—and praise from the ad community. Y&R might still have the account, had it not decided in 1985 to put the bull out to pasture.

It was a gamble; one that Y&R lost.

Y&R executives thought the bull was tied too closely to Merrill's past. They believed the bull told the world that Merrill Lynch Pierce Fenner & Smith Inc. still traded only stocks and bonds for retail customers, and that was no longer true. With the acquisition of White Weld in 1978, Merrill, long the largest brokerage firm, had become a leader in investment banking as well. It now raised money for corporations through the issuance of stocks and bonds, and had also become a force in the merger and acquisition whirlwind that would reshape the corporate landscape in the late 1970s and early 1980s. And Merrill had also moved overseas, becoming the first American brokerage house to gain a seat on the London and Tokyo stock exchanges.

To present the new Merrill Lynch, Young & Rubicam felt that new advertising was needed. That was the official explanation, but there might have been a more subtle motive. When they take over an account, the new advertising agency, as a rule, searches long and hard to find fault with the work of their predecessors. It is simply a matter of ego. "If the old agency's work was all that good, they'd still have the account," is what members of the new agency tell one another. To themselves, they say, "I'll be damned if I am going to use symbols and images created by someone else." It is not that hard to figure out why this happens. Creative people thrive on *self*-expression.

So Y&R replaced the bull—a symbol competitors say they would readily pay more than $1 billion to own—with a series of "docudramas." The ads showed clients with real-life financial concerns (putting a child through college; what would the latest turmoil in the Middle East do to the price of oil stocks they owned) and showed how Merrill Lynch could answer their questions and solve their problems.

The ads didn't work.

"Going into the campaign, we said to ourselves there is a good chance there's a great idea here, but the implementation is going to be tough," says Murphy, who is willing to share some of the blame for the failure. "But the initial research showed the concept was all right and on judgment we said it is worth the effort.

"As it turned out, the executions in almost every case got much too complex; they were hard to understand. The agency's theory was the details of the dramas were not important. What was important was that there was a problem, Merrill Lynch moved in and the problem was solved. They said whether anybody remembered anything else was irrelevant. You would be left with a positive image of Merrill Lynch.

"Well, what the agency and we—because we were involved in it—didn't fully recognize was the details got in the way of that message. There was too much information there for people not to be intrigued by it, yet at the same time they couldn't get it out fast enough to have it make sense. The viewer was left with no clear message. We did not succeed in creating either any new information registration with our clients, or potential clients, and we did not succeed in creating advertising that was exciting, that had breakthrough qualities.

"Our research showed it was all right. But all right is not good enough for Merrill Lynch, especially in the context of having this history of phenomenally good advertising. So we looked for another agency."

Presumably, the failures of the Y&R campaign could have been corrected over time, but Merrill Lynch didn't have time. Thanks to deregulation, it suddenly found itself in a much more competitive world. On one side, discount brokers such as Charles Schwab were capturing customers who just wanted to trade stocks and didn't want to pay for analysis from Merrill Lynch or anyone else. On the other side, huge competitors were entering the game, attracted by a new, deregulated environment. Suddenly it was possible to open financial supermarkets that offered one-stop shopping for everything from banking needs and insurance to financial planning and IRAs. The opportunities appeared limitless, and everyone wanted a chance to win big. In short order, Sears acquired Dean Witter; American Express bought Shearson, and Prudential Insurance gobbled up Bache Halsey. Virtually overnight, the most expensive and visible marketing battle that Wall Street had ever seen was underway, and in this environment, not only were Young & Rubicam's ads not helping, they were a liability.

"The whole category has gotten so cluttered with competitors that it was very difficult to break through to a relatively sophisticated audience," Murphy says. And worse, without the bull, the distinctive look of Merrill Lynch's ads was gone. It had become one of the virtually indistinguishable advertisers you'd see while watching television on Sunday afternoon.

"It had gotten to the point," says Murphy, "that if you were watching a golf match, you wouldn't be able to tell the financial-service commercials apart."

Of course this kind of advertising is not easy to do. You are trying to accomplish two things at once, and you have very few tools you can use to get the job done.

Your first goal is to sell a complicated product, an IRA account, a certificate of deposit, a municipal bond. And not only is the product hard to explain in 30 seconds, you can't even show it. All CDs and stock certificates look alike.

And that underscores the second problem, the one of differentiation. Not only do you have to explain what you are selling, you have to point out to consumers, who think all financial-services companies are the same, that your product is better than the other guy's. No wonder financial-service ads were terrible.

While there had been a couple of innovative ways to get the message across, there hadn't been many. John Houseman explaining that Smith Barney, recently acquired by Primerica, made money the old-fashioned way —"they earn it"—worked by telling investors something that they really believe deep down: There are no short-cuts to success. And if someone had told you E.F. Hutton does terrific research, you'd yawn. But by saying "When E.F. Hutton talks, people listen," Hutton got your attention. After that, though, you'd be hard pressed to think of another good financial-services ad. "You are trying to sell a complicated product to a sophisticated audience," Murphy says. "You are not selling Coca-Cola to everybody. You are talking about money, which is not an easy subject."

A $16-million gamble

Despite the inherent difficulties, once Murphy fired Young & Rubicam he found no shortage of agencies who wanted his business.

Part of the reason was the size of the account: Merrill Lynch spends a minimum of $50 million a year on advertising. While there are far larger advertisers—indeed, Procter & Gamble, RJR Nabisco and Philip Morris each spend more than $1 billion annually—Merrill is constantly among the leaders in financial-services spending.

But equally important to Madison Avenue was the high visibility the new campaign would provide. Careers had been made by doing good ads for Merrill. Just look at William Appleman, everyone said. Appleman, now 50, began his advertising career as a department store copywriter turning out such prose as "Bras, if perfect, $1.98, now 69 cents." But he will be known forever as the man who put the Merrill Lynch bull in the china shop when he worked at Y&R. That ad is a key reason he earns more than $350,000 a year.

Nobody was more aware of what the Merrill Lynch account could do to an ad man's reputation than David Bell.

Bell, vice chairman of Bozell Jacobs Kenyon & Eckhardt, was familiar with Merrill's advertising. Before Bozell bought his firm, Bell had been president of Knox-Reeves in Minneapolis, the agency that wrote the line "Wheaties, Breakfast of Champions." He ran Bozell's office in Minneapolis and then Chicago and was now, among other things, in charge of the $4 million or so which Merrill, Prudential Bache and Shearson were spending hawking their combined bond fund, called the Unit Trust Account.

So, long before the word was out that Y&R was in trouble, Bell had been studying the docudrama campaign.

"Candidly, I remember them more as an opportunity to do better than I remember them as a great epic in

American commercial making," Bell says, his hands behind his head, feet up on the cluttered conference table that doubles as his desk. "I think there were a number of problems. The biggest one being the startling absence of a symbol that had become as much a part of the corporate culture as it could possibly be." He pauses and then grins. "And besides, they were deadly dull and boring." Bell, tall, thin and partial to patterned shirts with contrasting striped ties, is never going to be accused of being self-effacing. And he knew he could turn out ads that were far better than Y&R was producing, given the chance.

But would he get that chance? Since Bozell was already doing the advertising for the syndicate that included Merrill Lynch, it was only natural that Murphy would allow Bell's agency to be part of the shoot-out—the industry's term for agencies doing battle for the same account. But, as excited as Bell was about Bozell being among the five agencies eventually chosen to compete, "we also had a problem" he says. "We were in the process of merging with Kenyon and Eckhardt and they had a very successful and productive relationship with a client called Pru[dential] Bache."

Not surprisingly, clients don't want their ad agencies working for competitors. So the choice at the newly created Bozell Jacobs Kenyon & Eckhardt was simple: stay with Pru Bache, or quit to go after Merrill. Keeping the status quo would be the safe course. Pru Bache was a $16-million account, and not only would Kenyon and Eckhardt be able to keep it after its merger with Bozell, the combined agency would also be allowed to retain the $4 million in Unit Trust billings, since Prudential was part of the trust syndicate. The alternative was to give up the $16 million in guaranteed billings, for a one-in-five shot at landing Merrill Lynch.

The question was taken to the board of directors. The decision? Let's go after Merrill. The size of the account was only part of the reason. The board, along with top management of BJK&E, felt that win or lose, competing for Merrill's business would truly bring the agencies together, since it would take all its resources to win the shoot-out. Besides, what better way to show the industry that Bozell Jacobs and Kenyon and Eckhardt had combined to create a truly powerful advertising agency—one capable of attracting any account—than going after and winning Merrill Lynch.

BJK&E told Murphy it was interested and, along with their counterparts from Grey Advertising, Dancer Fitzgerald Sample, NW Ayer, and Y&R—which had been given one last chance to save the account—BJK&E executives attended a series of briefings during which Murphy explained what it would take to become Merrill's advertising agency.

The message was simple; the assignment was not. To win the competition, an agency would have to prepare three sample ads which had the ability to break through the clutter of existing financial advertising, and which also accurately reflected what Merrill Lynch had become: an international financial institution that was as capable of selling stock to the little old lady from Pasadena as it was of preparing convertible subordinate debentures for the *Fortune* 500.

If the assignment wasn't daunting, the deadline was: Murphy wanted to see the ads in seven weeks.

And so began 49 days of endless meetings and 16- to

20-hour days. BJK&E's offices in an old department store on West 23rd Street, a less-than-fashionable area of Manhattan, were placed under siege. The agency turned its third-floor conference room into a makeshift cafeteria for the duration. Catered food was brought in at regular intervals and David Bell, backed by a cast of 200, set to work on what was clearly the biggest assignment of his career.

"We had to do everything simultaneously," Bell recalls, "and one step couldn't necessarily lead to another. In the real world, you might do all your research things, wait until the results were in and then spend two months synthesizing. When that was done, you would then formulate all your positions and spend another two months creating your advertising. That is a wonderful luxury and one we did not have. We had to do it all at once. While the research was underway, we were postulating hypotheses and strategies. We were looking at creative concepts twice a day—probably from 20 teams—for two weeks."

During these review sessions, Bell established the tone of the advertising BJK&E would present. He had sensed correctly during the briefings that Murphy was looking for commercials that would appeal to a viewer's intellect *and* emotions. That was exactly what Bell had been hoping to hear. "Our creative philosophy believes very strongly in the enrobing of simple, singular rational ideas in emotional clothing. By emotion, I am not talking about little kids and puppies. There are so many ads that you watch where you say, they are manipulating my emotions, but there is no idea behind what they are saying.

"What I am talking about is having a very clear central idea that is simple and easy to communicate and understand, and then executing it in a way that touches the feelings—either through humor, surprise, emotion, whatever—and in that process drives the rational thought deeper than it could be driven if it were driven rationally. That's what I mean by emotional advertising.

"We didn't hear Murphy say directly that he wanted emotional advertising. We felt it; we sensed it. And we believed emotionalism was required, given the fact that the docudrama work was nearly devoid of it."

The second key component Bell had decided to include was even more important. "It was not necessarily brain surgery, but we said the bull has to be in the ads, no matter what we did." It was the first thing people thought of when you said Merrill Lynch. And even though the symbol had been invented by others, it would be silly not to use it.

The bull's best angles

The question was how to bring the bull back. It took Bell a long time to come up with the answer. "We did everything from analyzing every piece of bull footage ever shot for Merrill Lynch, to employing a psychologist who literally had a specialty in understanding what the bull communicated to people."

The psychologist told Bell that some people saw bulls as being dangerous and unpredictable. But to most folks, bulls have a far better image. They're seen as determined, fearless and courageous—a strong, somewhat fearsome animal which is fully capable of taking care of himself.

That report eliminated any doubts Bell might have had about using the bull and he began studying the old Ogilvy & Mather and early Young & Rubicam footage, looking for ways to show the bull as strong, capable, competent and aggressive.

Bell runs a series of old Merrill Lynch ads to underscore what he did. "If you look at the bull sideways, or down, it looks dumb. It looks dumber than shit, if you want to know the truth. There is no majesty to it. There is no power to it. No aggressiveness." That could be deadly given what BJK&E found in interviewing typical brokerage-firm customers. Says Bell: "The research showed, interestingly, that unlike the competition, the Merrill Lynch customer was much more aggressive, much more self-confident, much more of a leader and much more authoritative."

If Bell had written the research reports himself, he could not have found a better justification for bringing back the bull.

"The real trick with using a corporate symbol is to capture the essence of what a company is and stands for and make that mesh with what consumers want, need and are looking for. The bull is just perfect for Merrill. When you marry the bull symbol to what we found in the research about Merrill's customers, you begin to see the relationship and the identity between the customer and the symbol."

And if customers perceive the bull as representing them symbolically, it becomes extremely important to ensure that the bull/customer is not portrayed looking dumb. Bell decided that every time the bull was shown, it would be shot either head on, charging toward the camera, or from underneath. Those were, in the words of Hollywood, "the bull's best angles." "This way the bull looks powerful, it stands tall and proud, there is a certain majesty about it," Bell says. "It communicates beauty and strength in a very nice way."

For far less, people have earned hundreds of thousands of dollars a year in advertising.

Bell had mastered the technique of using the corporate symbol. But he still didn't know what the copy should say—and the clock was ticking.

What would Cary Grant have done?

In *Mr. Blandings Builds His Dream House,* the best movie ever done about the joys of homeownership, Cary Grant plays a high-paid advertising executive who is able to buy an extremely expensive—although ill-fated—home in Connecticut thanks to his skill as a copywriter at the mythical firm of Baskin and Dantin. Throughout the movie, Grant wrestles with the slogan for his agency's most important account: Wham ham. He tries dozens of different approaches, from the direct ("Compare the price. Compare the slice. Take our advice. Buy Wham."), to the macabre ("This little piggie went to market/As meek and as mild as a lamb./He smiled in his tracks when they slipped him the ax./He knew he'd turn out to be Wham.") But nothing seemed to work.

After a desperate all-night session the day before the new advertising is due, a frazzled Cary Grant returns to his dream house, without having created a new campaign. Convinced he is about to be fired, he waits for the maid, Gussey, to serve breakfast.

When she finally announces it is time to eat, Gussey says, "We are going to have orange juice, scrambled eggs, and you know."

"Ham?" asks one of Cary Grant's small daughters.

"Not ham—Wham," Gussey replies. "If you ain't eating Wham, you ain't eating ham."

With that Cary Grant jumps up, kisses the maid, tells his wife to give her a $10 raise and rushes down to the office. The next shot is of the new print ads for Wham. They show Gussey holding a big platter of ham. The caption: "If you ain't eating Wham, you ain't eating ham."

Cary and family live happily ever after.

The real world, unfortunately for David Bell, was not so simple. While he had some ideas of what he thought a new slogan for Merrill should be, he waited to see what BJK&E's research showed about what potential clients of Merrill Lynch thought of the country's largest financial institution.

"Some of the research said that consumers were willing to grant Merrill Lynch supremacy on size, on depth of resources and capabilities," Bell recalls. "If they had concerns, they related to their ability to access that power.

"There is great strength in size, but there is also great weakness. The strength is that people tend to believe that larger [companies] may know more, but with that positive perception comes a burden of inaccessibility. Coldness. Institutional. Not warm, not friendly, not human, not real.

"In other words, consumers said, 'I know all those resources are there, but what does it mean to me? I understand big companies can get at those resources and use
them to make a lot of money, but how can I, the investor,
use them?' "

The customer wanted to know how to get at that power
and Bell wanted to know how to get to that potential
customer. One word was used over and over again, both
by the people surveyed, and within the high-ceilinged
rooms of BJK&E. The word was "harness." And it is a
word, says Bell, that "has a lot of virtue."

"It communicated in the genre of the Merrill Lynch
customer, i.e. it was authoritative, aggressive, strong, all
of those kinds of adjectives," Bell explains as he pauses
to sip from his ever-present diet soda. "It was also a word
that communicated that in the process of forming an al-
liance with the company, the customer would not lose
control. If I am going to harness something, I am going
to put it to work for me. Second, I am not going to lose
control of the son of a bitch, because I have it in a harness. And third, obviously I can access it. If I can put it
in a harness, then obviously, I can get at it."

If harness was a key word—and everyone agreed it
was—what would the Merrill customer be harnessing?
The answer was surprisingly simple: Power. "Power was
something that came back as a given with Merrill
Lynch," Bell explains. "You were willing to say Merrill
Lynch had power."

So the slogan would be "Harness the power." Bell was
particularly happy with it because, in the best tradition
of Cary Grant movies, it was a line he had written before
the research ever began.

To get the message across, the ads would show real people talking about their relationships with Merrill Lynch, and throughout their conversations, Bell would intercut images of a bull—charging, standing tall and so on. The bull would be back and the Merrill campaign would be personalized for the first time. The return of the bull would differentiate Merrill from the pack, and the use of real people would make a big financial institution seem a little bit warmer.

And so a great advertising campaign was born . . . almost.

"We ended up feeling very good and very smart about 'Harness the power,' " Bell says. "We thought we had a slogan that was remarkably flexible and could address a number of communication issues ranging from capital markets to planning for retirement. And because of our technique of intercutting the bull with people talking about their relationship with Merrill Lynch, it would communicate accessibility, humanity and emotion all at once. We thought we had what you could call an account-getter, as well as a hell of a good campaign."

But instead of organizing a victory party, Bell called everyone back together telling them that he appreciated their work, was proud of "Harness the power," and was sure it would win. He paused and added: "Let's see if we can do better." There were less than 25 days to the deadline.

Why would he do that? The slogan was terrific. The rough cuts of the ads looked wonderful. And everyone—Bell included—was exhausted. Why go further?

"When you have something you are comfortable with, if you are driven, professional and interested, you can do one of two things," Bell says. "You can say 'I've got it!' And you can look at it, walk around it, kiss it and leave it at that. Or you can ask yourself is there something we are missing? We went the latter route. We said okay, with 'Harness the power,' we've got it. Terrific. We are going to get the account, now what else can we do with it."

Bell and his staff went back to the briefing package Murphy had sent over and reexamined everything. They spent a lot of time rereading the sections on Merrill's corporate culture, and noticed again how the company was very proud of being the market leader and how it felt strongly that it had to set the standard for the industry.

You can see that just by looking at Merrill's position statement, where the company tries to explain to its clients and employees what it is and what it does:

> Merrill Lynch is a fully integrated investment and financial services firm, with extensive linkages among its consumer and capital market businesses. No other company can match Merrill Lynch for this kind of financial synergy—using its total resources to offer each and every client unparalleled professional advice and high quality, innovative financial products and services.

"After looking at those documents again, we said, You know what? 'Harness the power' is one of those things which is a wonderful street-fighting slogan," Bell says. "It is a wonderful opportunity for Merrill Lynch to battle head-to-head with all of its competition. But, we wondered, is there a high ground? A higher ground that transcends street fighting and takes you to a plateau that only a leader can find.

"There are certain responsibilities that leaders have,"

Bell says. "Leaders can paint with broad brushes. Second- and third-place companies can't do that. And we asked ourselves, is 'Harness the power,' really leadership? Does it really take the high ground and carry the emotional impact that a leader can generate?"

The Peebler connection

Bell is sincere in describing why he didn't quit with "Harness the power." But there was another reason that kept his staff working 18 hours a day, even after they had developed a solid slogan.[1] And that second reason went beyond an internal desire to do better.

Bell felt, and probably rightly so, that if BJK&E didn't win the Merrill account, the advertising industry would say Bozell—not Y&R—had lost it. That perception had nothing to do with creativity or ability; it had everything to do with friendship. It turns out that Chuck Peebler, chairman of Bozell Jacobs, and Merrill Lynch chairman, William Schreyer, are friends. That fact made some people wonder if the competition was rigged from the beginning.

It wasn't. You don't just blithely toss a $50-million account to a friend because he is a friend. Still, Bell was worried. Fond of gossiping about this sort of thing over long lunches billed to clients, Madison Avenue had made Bozell the odds-on favorite ever since Merrill announced its account was up for grabs. Its primary reason for doing so? The Peebler-Schreyer friendship.

1. Indeed, "Harness the power" would be used starting in late 1986 as the headline on ads for Merrill's capital-market group, the division that raises money for corporations.

So Bell felt compelled to keep working, if only to silence the skeptics. "We had to go beyond just good to win," he says. "Otherwise, everyone would have yelled, 'fix.' " As he went back and reviewed the briefing package, Bell kept asking the same question: Is "Harness the power" good enough? "The more we asked, the more we kept saying it is not. It is responsive, and responsible, but it really isn't high ground." It was, Bell would conclude, a bit too close to the kind of advertising already on the air, and that was not good.

"To say that all ads for financial-service companies are the same is an exaggeration, but it is more true than not true," Bell says. "You are dealing with a service business, so differentiation is difficult. There isn't a product that can be shown. Differentiation can be done, but it is difficult.

"And you are talking about a serious subject: money. So the tendency is to deal too much with the left side, the rational side, of the brain. That tends to lead you down much more boring paths. The traditional position is: 'You are talking about a lot of money here. Don't be fucking funny about someone's goddamn financial future.'

"I am not suggesting that flip is the way to go," Bell adds. "When you work only on the left side of the brain, with rational appeals, you are certainly following a safe course of action. But the downside is boring."

An ironic harness

In retrospect, the decision to go beyond "Harness the power" was a good one. During the finals of the competition, when all five advertising agencies presented their proposed campaigns to Merrill's board of directors, a strange thing happened. Dancer Fitzgerald Sample also unveiled "Harness the power" as its proposed slogan. While unexpected, the coincidence is easy to explain. Dancer had been given the same package of research materials from Merrill, had conducted the same kinds of research, and had discovered the same sorts of things Bozell had found.

But while its slogan was the same, Dancer's execution was different. There was no intercutting between real people and the bull. It was more straightforward than Bell's campaign.

In one DFS spot, shown in a closed-room screening to Merrill's hierarchy, a growing family is pictured at an ever-expanding dinner table while the narrator explains that the family was able to live well thanks to Merrill Lynch. Another execution begins with a close-up of three pretty sisters. They smile and you see each is wearing braces. The essence of the message: Thanks to Merrill Lynch's advice, their parents could afford the orthodontist's bills.

The ads were fine. But not particularly memorable, or innovative. Still, they had "Harness the power" as their slogan, and the board of directors liked the line. Dancer's presentation was still fresh in their minds, when it was Bell's turn to show what he had.

Not surprisingly, he was met with quizzical looks when he presented "Harness the power" and explained where the slogan had come from and how the executions would look.[2] "They were asking themselves, what the

---

2. Under the terms of the competition, the agencies were not allowed to shoot actual commercials. Merrill was trying to keep the agencies' costs down, having promised to pay each firm just $50,000 in expenses. So, instead of

hell was going on," Bell explains. "They had just heard this slogan from Dancer Fitzgerald."

It was then that Bell presented the winning entry. It turned out to be the mirror image of "Harness the power."

As the BJK&E staff went back over the company's history and old speeches, they kept playing with the concept of Merrill's limitless power and wondering what you could do with it. Sure, you could harness that power, but why not show how strong that power actually was. The first attempt to do that produced the line, "Merrill Lynch: Our world knows no boundaries."

"The line was very logical because Merrill was the first American firm on the Tokyo stock exchange, the first on London's, they are on the cutting edge of 24-hour trading, and blah, blah, blah," says Bell. "Their distribution and leverage worldwide made them formidable in any fields that involved international funding. They also were innovators in consumer products, such as the Cash Management Account [which allows customers to fund almost any investment, from the purchase of stock to retirement planning, through one account]. 'Our world knows no boundaries' plays well with all of that—and we changed it.

"After all, good advertising tends not to be introspective, it tends to be customer driven, benefit driven," Bell says. "It is far stronger if we keep all the substance of it, but turn it out toward the customer." The final version: "Your world should know no boundaries."

---

actual commercials, which would have far exceeded the $50,000 by themselves, the agencies presented animatics, slides which have been transferred onto film and are accompanied by a soundtrack.

In the movies, when someone first uttered the line, "Merrill Lynch: Your world should know no boundaries," Bell (played by Rock Hudson) would have screamed, "Eureka," kissed his loyal assistant, Doris Day, and champagne corks would have been sent flying throughout his second-floor office. It didn't quite happen that way.

"We didn't know for sure that 'Your world should know no boundaries' was better than 'Harness.' *We* thought it was, but until we tested it, we weren't sure."

What the tests showed was that although the words of the "Harness the power" campaign had changed, what made the concept appealing had not. In one execution of "Boundaries," as the campaign quickly became known, the Merrill Lynch bull—shot from slightly below to reinforce its majesty—is photographed throughout the world. He is shown trotting down Wall Street. Running along the sides of the Mississippi River with the St. Louis arch in the background, and out West. The background music for every "Boundaries" commercial would be the theme song from the James Bond movie, *For Your Eyes Only,* is heard. Now, however, the words have been changed to begin "To know no boundaries."[3]

Another ad, shot high in the Wyoming mountains, begins with a little girl of about six, well dressed and smiling, running through a field of wildflowers. She is quickly followed by another child and then by dozens of

3. Sung by Maureen McGovern, the lyrics were written by Bell and Robert Elgort, Bozell senior vice president and creative director. They are in part:

To know no boundaries, to let yourself run free.
To know no boundaries is what the world should be.
You can see so much in life, so much in life to do.
Now you see what the world can be.
To know no boundaries . . .

children of different races and costumes (hinting at Merrill's worldwide reach), and then by seemingly thousands of children—running, holding hands, playing with balloons. All the while the theme music is playing and the voiceover announces: "Whether you are investing for your future, or your children's future, your world should know no boundaries."

The ads were beautifully shot, striking and well received. Most of all they stood out against the rest of the financial-services advertising on television. Barbara Lippert, who reviews new campaigns for the trade publication, *Adweek,* describes them as "big, beautifully produced advertising. Everything—including the 1,800 pound bull—is on a massive scale. The bull running free, standing majestically or reflected in water gets the sort of lighting and camera angles a Bette Davis or Meryl Streep might covet."

The ads became a touchstone for Merrill's new approach to the market. The company used them as it began advertising through what BJK&E called "event media." As part of its new approach, the agency began searching for the opportunity for Merrill to become the sole sponsor of programs or magazines aimed at potential advertisers. Instead of being one of 100 ads that appear in a financial publication, Merrill's ads would stand alone. For example, it became the only advertiser of a special 53rd issue of the weekly *U.S. News and World Report* and the only advertiser on "Walter Cronkite at Large," a series of specials hosted by the former anchor of the "CBS Evening News."

There was nothing subtle about the approach. Ads promoting the Cronkite show, for example, carried the headline: "Walter Cronkite's world knows no bound-aries" and ended with "It all adds up to an hour nobody should miss, because it brings a whole new dimension to television. And makes it a world without boundaries."

But this direct approach worked. People started pay-ing attention again to the company's advertising. "This advertising is unlike any in the category and for that matter, unlike any that has been around," says a very proud James Murphy, who left Merrill Lynch in early 1987 to become executive vice president and managing director of corporate counseling and communication at Burson-Marsteller.[4]

"Television is a medium that needs emotion, in one form or another, to be effective," Murphy says, explain-ing the key to the new advertising. "It is not an intellec-tual medium. People don't watch television for analytical purposes, they do it for entertainment, primarily. You have to recognize that with your advertising.

"Just think of the campaigns that personally appeal to you," he continues. "They are humorous. There is an emotional tinge to them. Rarely, if ever, can you think of one that appealed solely to your intellect. So we needed a strong emotional appeal. And the production qualities, the settings, the music, all of it is being done to distin-guish it from the pack."

That sounds easy, of course. But Merrill faced re-straints that would not have hampered a packaged-goods company in creating new advertising. It couldn't show a fast-talking salesman—à la Federal Express—or the

4. The irony of that, of course, is that Burson-Marsteller is the public relations division of Young & Rubicam, the advertising agency that Murphy, in essence, had fired.

high tech wizardry that is routinely featured in commercials from Coke and Pepsi. Money, as Bell pointed out, is a serious matter. Here is where the decision to bring back the bull—a decision which on its face seems so simple—proved remarkably effective.

"The bull, when done right, can say volumes," explains Bell. "With the bull you have the symbol of strength, power, positiveness. That symbol not only dredges up all of the audience's feeling about the animal itself, but also the feelings about the way it has been used in the advertising. It recalls the original Merrill Lynch campaign— 'Bullish on America'—a campaign that was positive; that said America is up, we have a feeling of confidence. Like all symbols, it simplifies and amplifies the communication task and it takes the size of Merrill Lynch and its spectrum of financial services, and communicates in a way that is accessible, human and warm."

The bull acted as a bridge between the emotional appeal of little kids running through fields of wildflowers and the rational approach investors demanded. "Obviously, our strategy was to get the best of both worlds," says Murphy, unconsciously echoing the theme of Merrill's advertising. In other words, a world without boundaries.

3 | We got the juice: The importance of being different

Sometimes great marketing moves result from extensive research efforts. Then there is Slice.

If Brazil hadn't steadfastly tried to protect its juice industry, or if the Seven-Up Co. hadn't tried to market a cola, Pepsi might never have created the Slice line of soft drinks. Instead, it is more than likely that today a large portion of the country would be drinking Surf, another run-of-the-mill lemon-lime soda.

And, back in the late 1970s and early 1980s, that really was the problem facing executives at Pepsi's campuslike headquarters 20 miles north of Manhattan. The world just wasn't screaming for another lemon-lime soft drink. There were more than enough already. Seven-Up dominated, with more than a third of the category's sales. Coca-Cola's Sprite, with the "taste of lymon," was a distant second, but it still had a respectable 20 percent of the lemon-lime market. And Pepsi? Well, Pepsi had Teem, a perfectly fine soda, but the only place it sold well —for reasons nobody ever did figure out—was Buffalo, New York. Everywhere else, Pepsi executives conceded, the drink was a flop.

Since lemon-limes account for about 13 to 14 percent of the total $30-billion domestic soft drink industry, they are too big a market segment to ignore. And even if Pepsi

ROGER ENRICO of PepsiCo

executives wanted to write off the category, its bottlers wouldn't let them. They constantly told the company they wanted to sell more than colas and they suggested in no uncertain terms that the company produce a winning lemon-lime.

Faced with this mandate, Pepsi's research staff spent long hours staring at the Rodin, Calder and Miro sculptures that dot the grounds in Purchase, New York. Eventually they'd sigh and turn back to their beakers and Bunsen burners and continue their attempts to develop a lemon-lime that could beat Seven-Up in taste tests. If they could, Pepsi's marketing staff could do the rest. Given Seven-Up's overwhelming lead, coupled with the fact that soda drinkers are loyal to their brands (a fact Coke would learn the hard way), it was unlikely that their creation would ever be number one. But equaling Sprite's sales was possible. That wouldn't be terrific, but it wouldn't be anything to be embarrassed about either.

So, with more enthusiasm than hope, the research staff set out to develop a new lemon-lime soda. Code name: Surf.

And by the time Roger Enrico, a rapidly rising star within the company, became executive vice president and number-one aide to President John Sculley in 1982, Surf was ready for test market.

"It was a very good-tasting product, and had a very nice package, but I kept thinking, When consumers drink it, it is going to be Tweedle Dee to Seven-Up's and Sprite's Tweedle Dum," recalls Enrico. "There was nothing unique about it. You are always better off having a point of difference in your product, instead of just coming out with a me-too and relying on your merchandising and advertising ability. People in an industry as competitive as ours who say 'We are better marketers than our competitors, that's why we will win,' are just fooling themselves."

And Enrico wasn't about to try to fool anyone. "Surf was just another lemon-lime soda. We needed a point of difference."

But what? And that, frankly, had Enrico stumped. Then chance, and not great market insight, provided the solution.

As part of preparing him for a top slot within the organization, PepsiCo—the $8-billion parent company of Pepsi-Cola which also owns Frito-Lay, Pizza Hut and Kentucky Fried Chicken—had sent Enrico, although still in his 30s, to run divisions around the world. He had served as head of Pepsi's snack-food division in Japan and had spent a year running the company's soft drink operations in South America. "In Japan, the Coca-Cola Co. introduced the Hi-C trademark, but unlike here, where they sell through standard grocery channels, they had introduced it as a juice containing soft drink and sold it through bottlers and vending machines. And it was immensely successful.

"In South America, we—and everyone else—put juice in our flavored soft drinks. It had nothing to do with the products. It had to do with taxes. The governments there put value-added taxes on soft drinks. They are trying to protect their juice industry from the multinational soft drink companies. The taxes make traditional soft drinks more expensive, which in turn makes *their* juice more attractive.

"But if your soft drinks contain juice, you're exempt

from the tax. Since the tax costs more than the juice, there was actually an economic incentive to put juice in your lemon-lime and orange sodas. So we did. And my gut feeling was that the products tasted much better there than in any version I had tasted here."

And that included Slice.

"I was looking for some way of creating a lemon-lime with a hook, that would be different, exciting and have a reason for being," Enrico recalls. "And I was also wondering why the lemon-limes and orange products we had in South America tasted so much better."

A soda is born . . . almost

And then the light bulb went on. Pepsi would sell a lemon-lime soft drink that would contain juice. Neither Sprite nor Seven-Up had juice, so Pepsi's product would have the hook Enrico was searching for. And presumably, thanks to the juice, the soft drink would taste better.

A new product was born. Sort of.

Convinced he had a winning formula, Enrico figured that all he had to do was explain the concept to the head of Pepsi's research-and-development department and then wait for the sample. It wasn't that simple.

Flush with success in the late 1970s when it grew ever closer in total sales to Coke, Pepsi had—in the words of the growing number of business school graduates in its ranks—become risk adverse. The company, which created the Pepsi Generation and the Pepsi Challenge, just watched as Coke, under new chairman Roberto Goizueta, finally woke up. In short order, Goizueta's new team bought Columbia Pictures and then created Diet Coke, which quickly became the nation's third-best-selling soft drink, trailing only regular Coke and Pepsi.

What were Pepsi officials doing during all this? Patting themselves on the back and pointing back with pride at how far they had come. According to Enrico, nobody wanted to take chances. The head of R&D was representative of what was going on: "He was quite negative about my idea," Enrico remembers. "It couldn't be done. It would cost too much. The juice couldn't be preserved. We'd have manufacturing problems. You name it, he had it on the list.

"Then I got a brainy idea. I said why don't you go take a shot at it and if your guys can't do it, I'll hire Arthur D. Little (the consultants) to do it." With the message your job is on the line, a not-so-surprising thing happened. Enrico had a sample on his desk in a few weeks. "I tasted it and it was absolutely fabulous and then he told me it was the *diet* version.

"I remember grabbing the bottles and bringing them into Sculley's office. Sculley tasted it and said, 'This is the next big idea.' "

Flushed with success, Enrico ordered batches prepared and started selecting cities to serve as test markets. But when he tasted the first run, he was crushed. The soft drink didn't taste as good. "We never did duplicate those bench samples. I have never figured out what happened."

So, the research staff returned to their lab and Enrico and his staff thought some more about how you create a unique soft drink. And the more they thought, the more they became convinced that it was never going to happen.

It is one thing to say let's create a soft drink containing juice and then quickly whip up a sample in the lab. It is quite another to do it on a mass scale, when you have to take real-world considerations such as cost and availability of ingredients into account. Before you can even begin, there are all kinds of questions that must be answered, starting with the most basic one of all: What kind of juice do you use and, for that matter, how much do you put in?

"We did all kinds of concept work with focus groups, testing everything from 5 percent juice to 50 percent," Enrico says. "Below 10 percent, it was seen as meaningless. Ten percent was the hurdle rate, presumably established by products such as Hi-C [which stresses in its ads that it contains 10 percent juice]. People believed 10 percent juice would affect the taste. If you went to 15 percent or 20 percent, it didn't seem to give you anything. When you got into the 30 percent range, people began to see the product as something different. Ten percent meant you took some great-tasting juice, put it in a carbonated soft drink and what you got was a carbonated soft drink that tastes better. If you tell people you have 35 percent juice, they ask, 'Is that a juice or a soft drink or some kind of nectar?' Over 50 percent juice and people saw it as a juice with bubbles. So with 10 percent juice we thought we had the concept. We were borrowing some of the equities from the juice category—people think juice tastes great, they just don't think that it is refreshing—and trying to rub them off on a carbonated soft drink."

So 10 percent juice it would be. But what kind of juice? Certainly not 10 percent lemon or lime juices. After drinking that much citrus, you'd spend the rest of the day with your lips puckered.

"There were four factors in picking the juice," Enrico says. "When you are making a lemon-lime, it has to be clear. That is what people expect. That automatically put a restriction on the kinds of juice you could use. Then there were the issues of stability—both in taste deterioration and the product's turning brown. Cost—because obviously some juices are more expensive than others. And, finally, taste: You had to have a relatively neutral juice. One of the problems that I had perceived in the developmental process was that we were using an apple juice that was giving the product a very odd undertaste. It would drag you too far down on the crispness. We had to keep reformulating."

The company ended up using apple, pear, and grape juice, along with lemon and lime juice, and consumers approved of the mix. "They expected there to be some lemon and lime juice in there, but they didn't expect it to be the full 10 percent. We had no problem with consumers when we told them what juices were in it. That was something we worried about a lot. We didn't want to be attacked over what the juices were. Once you are attacked, you lose your credibility fast."

Credibility was an important issue. By adding fruit juice Enrico was giving the soft drink a patina of healthiness. And that, he clearly understood, was a two-edged sword.

By the time the soft drink entered test market in June 1984, "natural" and healthy products were all the rage —everything from chocolate-covered granola bars to certain kinds of potato chips were promoting themselves as "all natural," with the clear indication—usually false—that consuming them would be as beneficial as eating spinach. But Americans didn't seem to notice. They were growing concerned about their health and seemed to respond to anything that carried the words "lite" or "natural" on the label. Indeed, one of Enrico's orders to the research team had been to develop an all-natural soft drink, one containing vitamin C. It wasn't possible—it would have meant pasteurizing the soft drink which meant "you ended up with a crummy taste." Still, as Enrico says, by putting juice in the new soft drink, it acquired "a feeling of motherhood, a good-earth feeling."

The problem was, Slice was still basically a soda, and one with very little nutritional value. That was clearly spelled out on the can's ingredients list[1] but Pepsi still could be vulnerable if its marketing suggested, or even appeared to suggest, that the soft drink was "good for you."

"We were very, very careful, as we got into the marketing and the strategies, not to do anything that would imply naturalness or vitamins, because we didn't want people to say that these guys are bullshitting us. We obviously wanted to tell people about the juice, but we wanted to tell them it was 10 percent. That is important because nobody expected much in the way of nutrition when you said 10 percent juice.

"There is some indication that maybe I feel a little bit

1. Here, verbatim, are the contents of the soft drink: Carbonated water, high fructose corn syrup and/or sugar, blended concentrated fruit juices (apple, pear, grape, lemon and lime) citric acid, potassium benzoate (preserves freshness), potassium citrate, gum arabic, potassium sorbate (preserves freshness), salt, artificial color, glycerol ester of wood rosin, natural flavors, brominated vegetable oil, ascorbic acid and BHA (preserves freshness)

better about this product than I do about some others, but I don't think healthiness is a real selling proposition, and we haven't tried to exploit it because I think it would be making more of it than is there. When it comes down to it, the biggest reaction we get to the product is that it tastes better."

The problem was it also cost more. That isn't surprising since juice is more expensive than the flavorings used in traditional lemon-lime sodas. But, even though it wasn't surprising, it was a problem. The new soft drink was going to cost 20 cents more a case than a traditional lemon-lime, and in an industry as competitive as soft drinks, that, Enrico says, "is a lot."

"We had to wrap our minds around that, because we couldn't think of any practical way for consumers to pay for it," he explains. That being true, the question was who would absorb the cost? The bottlers, who buy the soft drink concentrate from Pepsi, or the company? Initially, Enrico had hoped to divide the cost along the lines of typical profit per case. He reasoned that, since bottlers have margins which are roughly double those of Pepsi, they should eat two thirds of the cost.

They ended up splitting. Says Enrico: "You have to be willing to put your money where your mouth is when it comes to the bottlers." It seems the bottlers liked the idea of having a new lemon-lime to sell, but they weren't crazy about making less money by selling it.

It will never fly

Convincing his superiors to endorse the product wasn't any easier. He needed $30 million to develop a product that would carry lower margins than a typical Pepsi soft drink. That is not the simplest way to get funding.

But Enrico thought he saw a way to pull it off. "There was a fairly good indication that the diet-regular mix here would not be normal. Normally, diet colas account for 20 percent to 25 percent of the total cola market. But it appeared that our new diet soda, because of its taste, would match the regular version in sales. Since we make more selling diet concentrate—the sugar substitutes are less expensive than sugar—we would be making as much on our new soda as we do on brand Pepsi. And who within PepsiCo is going to say Pepsi is a lousy business?"

No one. So, the soda made economic sense. And it was attractive for another reason—it made strategic sense as well. Not only would the new soft drink help Pepsi by finally giving it a strong lemon-lime to sell, it was also a way of getting back at Seven-Up.

Shortly after Philip Morris bought the Seven-Up Co. for $520 million in 1978, Seven-Up introduced Like, the first caffeine-free cola. Like was quickly outflanked by both Pepsi and Coke, who both introduced their own caffeine-free versions, but the memory of Seven-Up invading Pepsi's turf still rankled.

Up to that point, the unwritten understanding was that Pepsi and Coke would pay most of their attention to colas, and Seven-Up could have the lemon-lime market. "I'd never like to suggest that the real reason we got into this thing is because Seven-Up did the caffeine-free bit," Enrico says, trying hard not to gloat. "But I will tell you that it is not ridiculous to say that if they had never tried to come into the cola business, we might never have been so interested in being in the lemon-lime business.

"When they came into the cola category, that heightened our interest in lemon-limes and our focus on them as a competitor. We started thinking a lot more about Philip Morris, and wondering what their objectives were. Our reaction was not scientific, it is just human nature."

Enrico stressed both the advantages to Pepsi and the potential disadvantages to the competition as he pitched senior management for support of his idea. And he needed every argument he could think of, because his bosses didn't think the new soft drink would be a winner. They liked the concept, but they were convinced that Seven-Up and Sprite would quickly counter Pepsi's $30-million investment by introducing juice-enhanced soft drinks of their own—either by changing their formulas, or offering line extensions. Once that happened, Pepsi would once again have a "me-too" lemon-lime.

But Enrico didn't see that happening.

"If Sprite or Seven-Up were forced to put juice in to compete with us they would lose—God knows—30 to 40 percent of their gross profit," Enrico says. "And they would face two other problems. If you put juice in Seven-Up and Sprite, and you do it in such a way that it doesn't change the product, then you don't deliver on the juice proposition of tasting better. It still tastes like Seven-Up or Sprite.

"On the other hand, if you change the taste of Seven-Up or Sprite, a lot of people are not going to like it any more. They are going to ask, What have they done to my soft drink?

"And I didn't think they would line extend and offer a Seven-Up Plus, or whatever. I thought they would say,

'Wait a minute, a line extension is going to cannibalize my base brand [by drawing away existing customers]. And every time I cannibalize, I lose money.'

"I was convinced they were in a box. And when you are in a tough position, you tend to think very conventionally, because you really don't want to deal with it. Dealing in anticipation of your business being hurt is a very difficult thing. What you tend to do—and what I thought Coke and Seven-Up would do—is say, 'This is no big deal. It will never work.'"

Pepsi's senior management found Enrico's logic persuasive and gave him permission to spend $30 million that wasn't in his budget to introduce the soft drink, if he was sure it would sell. The problem was, Enrico still wasn't sure. All he had done up until this point was test the concept on a small number of people. Now he ordered extensive tests. "If the consumers didn't care, then this great hook idea was a zero. And this research told us very consistently that this concept had immense power. It appealed to the mainstream. It appealed to housewives as gatekeepers for their families, it appealed to larger families, you name it, and people—especially diet users—liked it.

"It had the ability to expand the market," Enrico adds. "Not because people thought that there was any particular nutritional value in a 10-percent juice soft drink, they just thought the juice would make the soft drink taste a lot better. So the idea of taking something which tastes great, like a juice, and putting it in a soft drink that tastes refreshing was a pretty close connect for them."

But it is one thing to come up with a terrific concept

that everyone likes, and it is another to fulfill the promise of a better-tasting lemon-lime.

It took almost a year. "We would go out and do blind taste tests against Seven-Up and we'd get killed. Then we would go back and mess around with the formula. It is not crisp enough, people would tell us, it is not tart enough, and then we change it. And then we go test it again and we would do better."

But the more the research staff fiddled with the formula, the closer the product came to tasting like Seven-Up. That would have been fine, except for one thing— people who said they were interested in the idea of a soft drink containing juice no longer cared. Sure, they said, the new soft drink contained juice, but it didn't taste better than Seven-Up. Thanks to all the tinkering, it tasted just about the same. And if it tasted the same, they weren't interested in switching. They'd drink Seven-Up.

Pepsi's product, as Enrico had originally feared, became Tweedle Dee to Seven-Up's Tweedle Dum.

It took Enrico a long time to understand what was going on, but he finally did. "When you give people blind taste tests, and they see two clear lemon-limes, they assume both are Seven-Up. The one that tastes different is the one they are not familiar with, and their initial reaction is they don't like it as well. People don't like change, unless they understand the reason for it. We finally figured that out. So, we started saying here are two soft drinks, one of them has 10 percent juice and the other does not, which do you prefer?"

Immediately, Pepsi's product started doing better, but it still wasn't a convincing winner. Why? Because changing the way you introduce it to people did nothing to change the fact that thanks to all the tinkering, what Pepsi had created was a virtual carbon copy of Seven-Up. No wonder it wasn't handily defeating Seven-Up. It *was* —for all intents and purposes—Seven-Up.

Enrico scrapped the revised formulas and returned to the original. And once people were told that what they were drinking was a new lemon-lime with 10 percent juice, the product sailed through the tests.

What do you call it?

That convinced Enrico he had a product he could sell. The problem was: What should he call it?

Surf was okay as a code name, but it was not particularly evocative of juice, or anything else for that matter. So Enrico launched a search for a new name. "We called in consultants and used computer-generated names but everyone has trademarked every damn word that has ever existed."

But there was an even more basic problem: When you are trying to come up with a name, be it for a baby or a soft drink, people tend to like only the names they think of. "Every time someone suggested a name, someone else said, 'That sucks.' It is so subjective," Enrico says. "It is the most unprofessional part of marketing. Maybe some people know how to do this well, but I have never been involved with them. And when you finally come up with a name that you like and you test it and consumers don't like it, you then say, 'What the hell do they know?' The truth is, consumers can't tell until they see it on a package."

Since there was no good way to test market names, everyone lobbied for his own favorite. And that included Enrico. He wanted to call his baby Sierra. It was a soft drink trademark Pepsi already owned and Enrico thought it conjured images of crisp, clear skies and sparkling water.

The name was terrific. But there were two problems. First, Sierra is a common trademark, and one that in fact belongs to the Sacramento-based Sierra Spring Water Co., a publicly held firm. Putting the name on a soft drink could lead to litigation. Problem two: Boss or no boss, nobody liked Enrico's choice.

What they did like was Slice, a trademark owned by Pepsi's Frito-Lay, which at one point had thought of using it to brand potato chips (as in a "slice" of potato). But Enrico hated the name. "It sounds strange now, because I am so used to it, but I just thought it was a dumb name for a soft drink. Yes, it was evocative of juice, you could think of a slice of fruit, so that was okay. But Slice?" As he says the name, Enrico wrinkles his nose as if he had just smelled a rotten banana.

"I wanted a name like Pepsi. Or Coke. Where are the consonants? I just didn't think Slice was real memorable. I wanted a name that didn't mean anything, so you could make it mean whatever you wanted to."

Sometimes that strategy works—most people don't seem to remember that Exxon is a made-up word—sometimes it doesn't. Changing United Airlines to Allegis in mid-1987 was universally ridiculed. But as Enrico said, there really is no good way of coming up with a name, despite what "corporate identity" consultants say. Everyone has his own opinion of what a good name

is and Pepsi's staff already knew Enrico's. He wanted
Sierra, so they did their best to keep him out of the nam-
ing discussion. That worked for a while but finally it
was time to show the soft drink's packaging to the ad
agency.

"I asked what name the product-development team
was going to put on the can," Enrico recalls.

"Slice," came the reply.

"No way," answered the head of Pepsi-Cola U.S.A. "I
am never going to put out a product from this company
with the name Slice on it. Forget it. I want Sierra."

The development team promptly ignored their boss
and went off and prepared package mock-ups that had
puffy, juicy-looking letters that spelled out Slice. "When
you saw it on the package, it looked fine," Enrico concedes with a shrug. "All my inhibitions went away. It
was clear that everyone at the agency and everyone on
the team wanted Slice. It looked pretty good and I wasn't
going to stand in the way of it. So we decided on Slice.
Now, in retrospect, I think Slice is a better name." Enrico
pauses and then smiles. "The name is probably less important than the amount of time we spent on it. Any one
of them would have been all right."

He may be right. When you put tens of millions of
dollars in advertising behind a product, what you call it
doesn't end up meaning very much, providing the name
is not ridiculous to begin with.

While there have been some truly terrible names created recently (Unum, Enron, and MBPXL are among the
worst[2]), most names end up being fine and after a while

2. Unum is the new name for an old insurance company: United Mutual
Life. Enron was what resulted when HNG and Internorth, two energy compa-

people stop thinking about their literal meaning. For example, when you hear Apple Computer, you think of innovative machines, not of a piece of fruit. Similarly, it is unlikely that you think of the incongruity of ordering chicken at *Burger* King. Given all this, Slice was a perfectly serviceable name.

So Slice finally had a name, formula and package. It was time to create the advertising. To do the work, Pepsi hired J. Walter Thompson, even though BBDO—which would bring the world spaceships beaming up Pepsi vending machines, and Michael Jackson swigging Pepsi and break dancing—had done its soft drink advertising until then.[3]

"BBDO had a very full plate with our Pepsi work," Enrico explains. "We selected Thompson, fundamentally, because they brought a different attitude about advertising to the party. Each agency has a different philosophy. Thompson's was: hardsell advertising you love to watch. I heard that line so many times I got sick of it. But, in fact, it was true. They were a very focused selling-proposition agency. If you have a segmented, targeted product, like Slice, you need to have a strong selling proposition."

Thompson had done hard hitting and effective advertising for Burger King (the series of ads that said "broiling beat frying," stressing the difference between Burger King and McDonald's hamburgers), and did the "Times

---

nies, merged. (Actually the name was to be Enteron, until a pundit realized that that was the name of a part of the lower digestive tract.) And while MBPXL looks like that line on the eye chart you can never quite read, it is really the name that was created when two Midwestern meat companies—Missouri Beef Packers and the Kansas Beef Industries—joined forces.

3. Pepsi would reassign the Slice account to BBDO three years later.

of your life" campaign for Kodak. Surely it would produce winners for Slice as well. That was what Enrico
thought. Then he saw the first ads.

"The worst ads I ever saw"

"They were terrible," Enrico recalls with a shudder. "The
meeting where we decided on the name Slice was also
the meeting where Thompson presented the storyboards
[the individual pictures that show some of the images
that will appear in the actual commercial]. The theme
line was 'We got the juice.' Well, I sure as hell didn't
have any problems with that. And they had a demo piece
of music that sounded pretty good.

"But they were doing a lot of talking about the imagery of this product and the kinds of people who should
be in these commercials. And frankly, I never understood
what the hell they were talking about. The people were
sort of hip, with-it, young people, but not kids. Young
adults on the beaches. Stylish. Very California," Enrico
says, groping to describe Thompson's pitch. "And they
kept talking about a new day dawning, that sort of thing.

"I kept saying there is no way you can do this in the
context of a 30-second commercial. You have to get
across 'We got the juice' and you want to put some juice
and refreshment feeling into it and show the product,
and you keep talking about wanting to play up the idea
of a new day dawning. It ain't going to work."

But after several meetings with Thompson where he
voiced his concerns, Enrico gave the go-ahead to the commercials the ad agency had presented. "I walked out of
those meetings with the feeling that they were telling

me that, 'Look, we know how to produce advertising.'
And I said to myself, Maybe we are treating them like
children, like we don't trust them to do great film. So, I
thought we ought to let them go with it."

So Enrico waited until Thompson called to let him
have a look at the rough versions of the spots. Everyone
gathered in a small conference room at Pepsi's headquarters. "The videotape rolls and this stuff is awful. It has
the makings of something, but it is awful. For example,
the singers would say Slice, and you are looking at the
moon or something. Then the can would come on and it
was turning, so you never did quite see the entire logo. I
wouldn't have cared as much if this was Pepsi, but this
is a brand name no one has ever heard of before.

"And they had cast this thing with some of the weird-
est-looking goddamn people I had ever seen in my life. I
have no idea where they got them. They were not attractive. The boys were very effeminate. A little greasy. It
was almost a campy thing. It had to be a style out there,
but it wasn't the way you saw kids looking around the
country. I couldn't stand them. The entire imagery didn't
work.

"Now this happens a lot. You look at film and it is not
edited right. Usually when we do a commercial you shoot
so damn much film, you don't have to worry if you don't
like the first edit. The agency has miles of film and they'll
go back and edit it again. I didn't know if they had more
film or not on this one." And Enrico really didn't care.

When you are introducing a mass market item—especially one like Slice where you are worried about being
quickly copied by the competition—you want to establish
your position fast. That means using television to get

your message across. Your commercials must be effective, and clearly Thompson's were not.

"I got really mad because of what I had told them when we discussed the storyboards. I told them it was about the worst advertising I had ever seen. I was pretty rough on them. I think I gave them three days to get the ad in the can. That must have been midweek. We went down there on a Saturday morning into Manhattan into an edit studio. I will never forget walking in, the top brass of Thompson were all there."

There was no small talk. "They went right to the movieola. They had actually shot more product footage, and reoriented the thing. They put normal drink shots in it, forgot the people really, and concentrated on product imagery. It looked great. I was very pleased."

He had reason to be. In just 30 seconds, Thompson managed to get across the key facts about Slice, and did it entertainingly.

For example, all the initial spots—which featured a rock and roll soundtrack behind young adults dancing, engaging in gymnastics or practicing karate—go out of their way to mention the competition. The Seven-Up and Sprite buttons on a vending machine are shown as you hear the lyric "We have the juice that Seven-Up and Sprite have missed."

That simple line accomplished three significant points. First, it told people that Seven-Up and Sprite, contrary to what many consumers believed, didn't contain juice. "They didn't know how much—and they thought it was probably less than 10 percent—but the research showed a lot of people thought they both had juice," Enrico says. "By pointing out that Slice did have juice, it not only got the product's distinguishing feature across, it also underscored the significance of it." Says Enrico: "If we didn't say, 'We have the juice that the others have missed,' a lot of people would have said, 'Big deal. Lemon-limes are supposed to have juice.'"

Second, coupling the line with the shot of the vending machine buttons instantly put Slice in the right competitive context. You didn't have to spend time explaining that Slice was a lemon-lime soft drink. Comparing it to Sprite and Seven-Up did that for you.

Finally, saying that juice was what "Seven-Up and Sprite had missed," implied that Slice was better than its competition.

It was an effective introductory spot.

Product in hand, advertising in place, it was time to roll Slice nationally—or as far nationally as Enrico could. Slice had a distribution problem, one that still hasn't been solved. It is a problem which can be traced directly to Teem, and is complicated by the nature of the soft drink industry.

Pepsi bottlers are not Pepsi employees. They, like Coke bottlers, are independent businesspeople. They run their own companies, many of which are publicly held. Their relationship with Pepsi is a contractual one. Pepsi promises them an exclusive territory in which to sell its soft drinks and the bottlers promise not to sell competing products. If you sell Coke, you can't sell Pepsi.

That makes sense. But there is nothing in that contract that requires bottlers to carry every part of Pepsi's line, and faced with the slow sales of Pepsi's lemon-lime Teem, about 20 percent of Pepsi's bottlers had decided to sell Seven-Up instead. They signed separate agreements with Seven-Up, and one of the conditions was that they couldn't sell a competing lemon-lime. And Slice clearly was competition.

At some point, those Pepsi bottlers might choose to stop selling Seven-Up, but that wasn't going to happen immediately. No businessperson is going to drop the market leader for a sight-unseen challenger like Slice.

Lacking 20 percent of Pepsi bottlers for the Slice roll-out was "a problem," Enrico concedes, "but what am I to do as a result, ignore the lemon-lime market?"

A second problem flowed from the first. Lacking national distribution, national advertising didn't make sense. National ads would air in places where Slice wasn't sold.

So Slice would be introduced through "spot market" advertising—television time would be bought on a market-by-market basis. It costs about 10 percent more to buy time this way, but when you are spending $28 million on an initial advertising blitz, as Pepsi did in late 1984, that really doesn't amount to much.

"We got to the $28 million figure by looking at the second-tier soft drinks—Diet Coke, Diet Pepsi, Seven-Up —and they were in the 30-millionish range," Enrico explains. "We had spent at least that much to get some attention."

And getting attention, even within the PepsiCo family, was going to be difficult. Enrico introduced Slice to the bottlers at the same 1984 convention where he unveiled the first Michael Jackson commercials.

His initial thought was not to talk about Slice at all. "It was too early, we wouldn't be going into test market for several months, and I did not want to tip our hand competitively," Enrico says. But the *Wall Street Journal* gave him no choice. Right before the bottlers' convention, it published a small story that outlined the entire Slice campaign. The 10 percent juice, the tag line—everything. "After the article, there weren't any secrets anymore," Enrico says. "So I told the bottlers what we were working on and showed them the commercials.

"I went to great pains to say I didn't know if this would be the greatest thing since sliced bread—no pun intended. I told them we go to test markets in four months, and if it works, then we would be back to see them."

Why downplay the first new major soft drink name since Coke rolled out Tab some 20 years before? "I wasn't prepared to do anything other than take Slice to test market," Enrico replies. "And as long as all I am going to do is test it, there is no point in getting the whole world excited. Everything looked like it was all right, but the proof of the pudding is in the testing. I just didn't feel I was in a position of taking the financial risk, or quite frankly the credibility risk, to roll an idea nationally out of consumer research, put 30 million bucks behind it and have it fail, or not be a resounding success— it wouldn't have failed."

"That was number one. Number two, we had a couple other more important priorities. We had to get Pepsi rolling. Pepsi is two-thirds of our business and we had to get it rolling. Three, we were being killed by Diet Coke. We had to get it going. So just in terms of priorities, Slice had to fall down."

But it didn't fall down in Phoenix, Rochester or Tulsa, the three test markets Pepsi picked. The repeat business was excellent and the diet business "was better than we anticipated. It was half the business, so obviously you had something big here. Take the juice away, take the advertising away, and you still had a terrific diet product. That gave us even more confidence."

Somewhere over the rainbow

And it also gave Enrico more confidence in the concept. "As we went out and saw the acceptance of Slice, and saw the repeat business and the amount of news it generated, we started to get the feeling that this was a lot bigger idea than just a lemon-lime. The hook was not a lemon-lime with a difference. It seemed to be a soft drink that contained 10 percent juice. If that was so, Slice would become extendable to other flavors, as long as we put the juice in each one."

Until this point, Enrico had been toying with the idea of line extensions, samples had been worked up, but only "to keep our bases covered."

"We started getting serious about Orange Slice as we went into 1985," he adds. "But I was very torn between extending Slice and not extending it." The bottlers didn't face this dilemma. They hated the idea of line extensions. "They felt Slice should stand for a lemon-lime," Enrico recalls. "And they would lecture me that nobody has been successful in the rainbow business."

A rainbow brand is one that has a name in common and little else. While Pepsi might sell Diet Pepsi, or Pepsi Free, you know that if you see the Pepsi label you are buying a cola. With a rainbow brand, you have to read further. Shasta is a good example. The Shasta name is on everything from a cola to a lemon-lime to a root beer.

Pepsi bottlers repeatedly told Enrico that having Slice's name on more than a lemon-lime would confuse people and ultimately dilute its success. "My counterargument, even though I hadn't made up my mind yet, was that I thought the hook really was the 10 percent juice," Enrico answered. "If that was the case, then people won't be confused. The Slice name will stand for good-tasting soft drinks that contain 10 percent juice. We'd have the ability to line extend."

Some preliminary research proved him right. "When we tested the Slice concept, we also said we have an orange, or an apple, and people would say, 'Great! Now my friend who doesn't like lemon-limes can drink a product with the juice, because he really likes the idea of juice in soft drinks.' People didn't see it as a disconnect. They said they would like to see the juice in a broader variety of flavors."

But that was just in abstract testing. Wary that the bottlers were correct in thinking consumers would be confused if he added another flavor, Enrico ordered extensive testing of Orange Slice. "We went through the same drill we did with the lemon-lime, matching it up with Orange Crush and Sunkist. Finally we are comfortable with the way it tastes and we test it in Hartford and Phoenix. Now I don't have to see any more. It just walks off the shelves. The orange outsells the lemon-lime, and that continues to be true. Now all the intellectual arguments and all the theories are gone. People aren't confused. By adding the orange, we were reinforcing the fundamental selling proposition. As a result, we have doubled the business. That means we can spend twice as much on advertising. That is when I got interested in building the Slice trademark."

There were two reasons Enrico wanted to expand. First, he wanted to cut off competition. Given the success of Orange Slice, he knew everyone from Orange Crush to Sunkist might soon be adding juice and "we expected Coca-Cola's Minute Maid [orange soda] to become competitive any day. Second, I did not want a repeat of the Pepsi Free experience.

"With Pepsi Free [Pepsi, without caffeine], we were the lead guy out in the marketplace, for all practical purposes.[4] When Coke came in with a caffeine-free later on, we initially outsold them two to one. But that began steadily narrowing and the advantage we should have had by being out almost a year before them didn't sustain itself. I didn't want to have that happen with Slice. I almost became paranoid with the thought that all we'd end up with was kudos for creating a new category. Who the hell cares about that? You can put it on your résumé, but who cares?

"I wanted Slice to be like Doritos," Enrico adds. "Frito-Lay took tortilla chips, called it Doritos, put it out there and today Frito-Lay accounts for 80 percent of all the tortilla chips sold in the U.S. Tortilla chips are almost Doritos in consumers' minds. That is what I wanted Slice to be."

To keep the attention both of his bottlers and of the

4. That was true. While Diet Rite Cola and Seven-Up's Like created the market, Pepsi quickly became the market leader after it introduced Pepsi Free.

public on Slice, Enrico ordered Apple Slice and Cherry Cola Slice rolled out without test marketing.

Cherry *Cola* Slice?

Introducing Apple Slice was a relatively easy decision. "We felt this was a great product. We thought it tasted better than apple juice, and would probably be a sleeper. It might start off pretty modestly, but would grow, thanks to word of mouth."

Cherry Cola Slice was another matter. "It was not something we had even considered when we thought about new flavors for Slice," Enrico says. "But we had Cherry Coke out there, and we assumed that Diet Cherry Coke would be coming. Cherry Coke had gone out with a splash, and we were concerned about it. There was a great deal of pressure coming from bottlers and some of our own employees who felt we ought to have a Cherry Pepsi."

To counter Coke's threat, Enrico's research department developed a Cherry Pepsi,[5] and it beat Cherry Coke in blind taste tests. Still, Enrico was not convinced.

"I didn't want to line extend Pepsi. I didn't want to diffuse the effort behind Pepsi and what it stood for. I had done it with the Pepsi Free, but that was just Pepsi without caffeine. I said to myself, We can put out Cherry Pepsi and beat Cherry Coke in blind taste tests. But there is nothing particularly distinctive about it. And while I figured we would probably have a success, I

---

5. Pepsi's international division was already selling a Cherry Pepsi in Canada and England that had been well received.

thought the cannibalization of brand Pepsi would be very high."

But what would happen, Enrico wondered, if he responded to Cherry Coke by introducing a cherry-cola form of Slice? He is quick to answer his own question. "We'd one-up Cherry Coke, albeit we'd be starting from a much lower base of brand awareness, but we'd have a point of difference. We'd have 10 percent juice. Strategically, Jesus, that sounded pretty good. We could kill two birds with one stone. We could be in the ball game with Cherry Coke, have a product advantage, and at the same time keep Pepsi pristine."

There was a problem. Cherry Cola Slice was different from any of the versions that had come before. It was a cola, not a soft drink based on a fruit flavor. "We did think maybe the *cherry* in cherry cola would help a little —since it did contain a fruit," Enrico says with a laugh. "But that of course was the big question. Was this an absolute disconnect for consumers?

"We did some pretty extensive testing with consumers and while it wasn't the strongest of flavor concepts we have ever put out, it was strong enough. In the focus groups, the fact that it was a cola didn't bother people. They said, 'A lot of us like to drink colas and having cola with 10 percent fruit juice makes a lot of sense. We think it would be more refreshing.' So we talked ourselves into doing it."

It is an apt choice of words. Cherry Cola Slice has struggled in the marketplace. While lemon-lime is doing about what Enrico expected, with about 3 percent of the total market, and orange far exceeded expectations and has close to 4 percent, cherry cola—along with apple—are limping along.

"We have got other flavors on the shelf, and what I see us doing, if one looks like it is not going to be a legitimate contributor to the line, is swapping it right out. We'll put ABC Slice on the market, and take Cherry Cola Slice out. We don't have to do that nationally. We can do it market by market. We can deal with 20 percent of the country having Cherry Cola Slice and 20 percent having apple. We don't care if we are advertising the Slice trademark. But I don't want a Pepsi Light [the ill-fated Pepsi with a lemon twist] situation, where there is a long, lingering death."

It is interesting to note how Enrico has defined the future. He has no immediate plans to add more flavors. He is taking great pains to insure his lead. "We have a lot of homework to do. We have low awareness of cherry cola. We have lots of distribution voids. Slice, for example, is only tied in on Pepsi displays 25 percent of the time right now. That means there are somewhere around one million temporary Pepsi displays that we haven't put it on yet. There are lots of basic things like that we have to do. We still haven't leveraged the merchandising power of the system behind Slice. It takes time.

"I do think we will end up getting a respectable share of this category but, by respectable I would hope Slice would have three times the share of its competitors. But I don't think the way to do it is by adding more flavors. When you grow something this quickly, you are almost skimming the surface and you want to get down deep." Enrico wants to make sure Slice takes full advantage of

Pepsi's marketing power and uses its promotional budget to reinforce the image of the existing flavors. "I would rather have us focus on that. Eventually the brand has got to grow of its own accord, instead of adding new flavors."

How big can it grow?

"Well, we set a goal—admittedly I pulled it from the air but I think you ought to set high goals—a 10 share [of the total soft drink market] or $3 billion in sales. That's a high goal. But where we have all four flavors, we have over a 7 share."

It *was* a big idea

Enrico can dream of $3 billion in annual sales because Slice was a big idea. But why?

"Not because of the perceived nutritional value of juices, but because people thought the juice would make it taste better—and that, in fact, it did. The product delivered against the concept, and demonstratively so, in the diet. It is that simple."

Not quite. Serendipity played a major role in Slice's success; so did the debacle that will be known forever as "new Coke." Of the two, serendipity is probably more important.

As we have seen, Enrico is a firm believer in extensive market testing. But had Pepsi not sent him to either Japan or South America, the odds are quite good that his research department would never have had the concept of a fruit-flavored soft drink to test. The tour in South America is where Enrico learned about putting juices in soft drinks and the stint in Japan is where he saw Coca-Cola's success with selling Hi-C, containing fruit juice, as a soft drink.

Coke was to help Slice in yet another way. About the same time that Enrico's staff was working to develop the product that would be known as Slice, chemists at Coca-Cola's Atlanta offices were working on what Chairman Goizueta would call on April 23, 1985 "the surest move in its 99-year history"—the introduction of new Coke.

The preoccupation with developing new Coke—you don't blithely go changing the formula of the world's best-known soft drink—and the resulting firestorm caused by its introduction, completely occupied Coke's top management at the very time Slice was being rolled out. When Slice went into test market in 1984, Coke executives were still debating the wisdom of changing Coca-Cola's taste. Slice was already available nationwide by the time Coke executives were agonizing over bringing old Coke back.

In effect, Coke gave Enrico a more-than-two-year headstart—a virtually unheard-of lead time—in what the business press is fond of calling the "soft drink wars."

And Pepsi took advantage of that time to create a new soft drink category—juice-enhanced soft drinks—and to establish Slice as the market leader.

Coke's preoccupation gave Enrico time to do extensive consumer testing, but ultimately the decisions of what Slice would taste like would be made by a group of people sitting in his office tasting samples.

"I don't want to put down the amount of effort that went on in the R&D in developing these products; it was a lot. Don't forget, we didn't know anything about juices, and especially not about the application to carbonated soft drinks. So there was a whole hell of a lot of technical work that went on. There were more man-hours spent in R&D developing lemon-lime Slice than there had been spent on all product-development projects the entire prior year.

"But I am convinced that you cannot build a product out of consumer research. There isn't any consumer research that is so precise as to tell you what to do on every particular characteristic. The science isn't there, number one. And number two, the consumers don't care nearly as much about this product as you do. It is hard for them to articulate and then it is hard for that articulation to be translated back into something you can read. Any time you are building a product only on numbers—even though numbers are very important—you are going to get into big trouble.

"I think the reason Coke got into trouble with new Coke was that they looked at all the blind-testing numbers and said consumers prefer this new thing to our existing formula. But consumers were just drinking little sips. And I don't care if you did ten million tastes, they never told the people that if they liked new Coke they were going to take old Coke off the market. They never asked, 'What do you think of that?' If they had, people would have asked, 'Are you nuts?'

"I wouldn't want to give you the feeling—because it isn't true—that we are this terrifically instinctive group that wings it and hits the bull's-eye more often than not. We do lots and lots and lots of consumer research. And by the way, we don't only do it when we are testing something. We do it on a consistent basis. The more data you get coming in on a regular basis, the closer you are to the consumer, the better your judgment is going to be when you have to make the call without having data on a specific issue."

Like when you are trying to invent a different product.

Zap! You're it!: How to build a successful product

Paul Rago swears he never cheated at tag. Growing up in suburban California, tag was a favorite game with kids in the neighborhood and Don Kingsborough claims Rago, now his partner and, for more than 30 years, his friend, constantly cheated.

"He'd say I only got his shirt or his pants and my tag didn't count," Kingsborough recalls. "He never wanted to admit he was 'it.' "

That was back in the mid-1950s. Some 30 years later, in early 1985, Kingsborough, Rago and other key members of the company that had created the phenomenon known as Teddy Ruxpin, were sitting around Kingsborough's pool trying to figure out what they should do next. Judging by the toy buyers' response, Teddy, as it is affectionately known by Worlds of Wonder's corporate officers, was going to be a huge hit. Indeed, Worlds of Wonder would sell $93-million worth of the bears in 1985. The problem was what to do for an encore.

That was the reason for the poolside meeting. Kingsborough, chairman of Worlds of Wonder, had invited key members of his staff to his home to discuss new products. They started by talking about the games kids liked to play, and soon they were recalling childhood memories.

DON KINGSBOROUGH of Worlds of Wonder

That's what prompted Kingsborough to start kidding Rago, now his vice president of marketing.

But the kidding—and all the rest of the discussions—stopped when Rago asked a question: "What if we could solve that problem of knowing when you are tagged?"

"Paul then began to describe the concept of Lazer Tag, a game where you shoot a beam of light across great distances to 'tag' another person. We instantly knew the concept was great," Kingsborough recalls. "And right there at the pool we started sketching what the product would look like. Within a few hours we had a real good idea about what Lazer Tag would be about and how it would work."

It sounds haphazard, but that casual, poolside conversation was part of a very structured approach Kingsborough uses to create new products. He refers to it as a templet, and every product Worlds of Wonder—a name Kingsborough chose because he wanted his company to be known as WOW in the stock tables—must fit into the model. If it doesn't, no matter how intriguing it is, Kingsborough won't sell it. For a man whose huge corner office is littered with toys, and who has been known to hold meetings at the patio table on the small deck outside the sliding doors to his office, such structure appears incongruous. But it works. Worlds of Wonder racked up $320 million in sales in its second year of existence, a feat believed to be the fastest start ever recorded by a public company.

It was, of course, a pace that could not be maintained. As we will see, there was nothing wrong with the business plan that produced this remarkable growth. The problem was adhering to all the details of that strategy.

The strategy begins with two basic tenets. First, Worlds of Wonder will only produce toys that children already play with or would like to play with. Consider Teddy Ruxpin. Children like teddy bears. You don't have to explain to them what a stuffed animal is, or why they should love it. But producing just a teddy bear is no guarantee of success. That brings us to Kingsborough's second rule. Having discovered something children already like, WOW will improve it by adding technology that has never before been used in a toy. With Teddy Ruxpin, the technology allowed the bear to "talk."

Technology also allows Kingsborough to fulfill the second part of the templet, which has four parts:

1. Make a great product. The technology allows him to do just that.

2. Do great advertising. The technology gives Worlds of Wonder's toys easily distinguishable characteristics that can be stressed in ads. A talking teddy bear is something that will grab your attention.

3. Do great public relations. When you have a unique product, it is easy to get people talking about what you have.

4. Have exciting retail displays which underscore why your product is unique and which are tied in with the advertising.

The final section of the templet has two parts, both designed to protect the advantage that Kingsborough says you will have if you follow the first part of the strategy.

First, you must extend your product as far as you possibly can through licensing arrangements and add-ons. Second, knock yourself off before the competition can.

Teddy Ruxpin begat talking Mother Geese, Snoopys, Mickey Mice and the like.

Kingsborough was just starting to develop this strategy—although he could not yet articulate it—when he stumbled upon Teddy Ruxpin in February 1985.

As the former head of Atari's consumer products division, and a long-time consultant, Kingsborough was well known in the industry. So it wasn't surprising that Teddy's creators—the people at Alchemy II, a small company in Northridge, California, that specializes in developing toys that it licenses to others—would give him a call about their new product. A call that came only after virtually every major toy company had already turned them down.

But even though he was last in line, Kingsborough wasn't miffed. He took one look at Teddy and said "the big companies are missing the boat. This is a winner. They just don't understand what it is."

Where the major toy companies went wrong, Kingsborough would explain later, is that they thought a stuffed teddy bear who talked and sang songs was yet another technology product. And if that is how they saw Teddy, the rejection made sense. The major toy companies were already stuck with more technology-based gizmos than they knew what to do with.

In February 1985, when Kingsborough first saw Teddy, the toy industry was still trying to recover from the electronic-game debacle. Starting with "Pong," demand for video games that went "whir," "biz" and "pop" soared and the industry spent hundreds of millions gearing up for a market that they dreamed would last forever.

It didn't. That isn't surprising. In the toy industry, a toy is considered an "evergreen" (i.e., a classic) if it sells well for five years. Electronic games never made it into that most-valued category. And when demand for Pac Man and his kith and kin dropped off nearly as quickly as it came, the industry was stuck with warehouses-worth of inventory that it was giving away. Literally.

Just at the time that Kingsborough was meeting Teddy, it was possible to buy a video game for nothing. Retailers were offering some games for just $5 *and included with the game a $5-rebate offer.* If you sent the form in, you got all your money back. No wonder the last thing the industry wanted to look at was a teddy bear that came with a circuit board.

"The toy companies had been blown away in the video-game business," Kingsborough sums up accurately. "Coleco, Milton Bradley, Mattel had all suffered greatly. The result was they were absolutely frightened away from technology, and that is how they saw Teddy. They saw him as a technology gimmick, and they were now afraid of technology.

"But what they missed as a result of that fear was that kids were already predisposed to like animated characters. They had been to Disney World [where, among other things, the Country Jamboree features life-size singing and dancing bearlike characters]. They had been to pizza parlors [like Chuck E. Cheese, that featured animated, anthropomorphic critters who sing and tell jokes] and all they needed was someone to provide this sort of thing for them at home. To kids, Teddy was not a technology product, it was an animated character, something they already liked. The other toy companies missed its meaning."

They did, but Kingsborough didn't. After all, it fit in perfectly with his templet for success. And if it worked with Teddy, Kingsborough figured, it should work with whatever he introduced in 1986. So he and his staff began looking for a second toy—something kids already knew about and one Worlds of Wonder could improve with technology.

"Kids understand technology, and most industries— medical, auto, computers—had been touched by technology in some way. Most industries, but not toys. Toys were always molded plastic. It seemed to me that technology could change this industry.

"What I said to myself from the beginning was it looks like there is a place for a company that can translate technology from other industries to kids' products. To take what kids think, imagine and dream about and make it more into reality for them. That's what we could do. We would become a company that simply translated technology from other industries to the consumer-products industry. It couldn't be state-of-the-art technology. It would have to be a step back from that so we could do the translation at low cost. But it still would be technology that the toy industry didn't have.

"It seemed very logical to me. There wasn't anybody else doing it, they were afraid of it. It was a market niche."

Buck Rogers, Luke Skywalker and me

And so, as they sat around the pool, Kingsborough's staff shared a common starting point. They were to create a toy that used technology employed by other industries. But there was something else implicit as well. Remember, when Kingsborough talks about applying technology, he means applying technology to improve something kids already do—like play with stuffed teddy bears—or have dreamed about doing.

"I always like to sell items that the consumer already knows about," Kingsborough says. "If somebody already knows about it, and enjoys it, the risk is not nearly as great as if you are introducing a product that they have never heard of before. What we want to do is provide function and style to things they already do, as opposed to creating something we have to teach them how to do."

In that sense, Teddy Ruxpin was just a home version of Disney World's Country Jamboree bears or a smaller, portable version of the characters they had watched sing songs at the fancy pizza parlor down the street. And Lazer Tag?

"Kids have seen *Star Wars*, but the appeal of Lazer Tag really goes back to the Buck Rogers serials," Kingsborough says. "Kids had been wanting this their whole life. Now the technology was available and you could do it at a reasonable cost."

But what was "it" exactly? Rago had sketched out a gun that would shoot a harmless beam of light across great distances. Fine. But there were two vital questions. Could you actually build the toy inexpensively, and in

Kingsborough's words, "still make it as cool as we wanted it to be?"

And even if you could, exactly what would kids do with it? The concept, after all, was tag. How would kids know when the beam of light connected?

The technology question turned out to be simple to answer, even if it took Kingsborough and his staff a while to figure out that they were approaching the problem backward. Initially they spent most of their time and effort studying the gun itself. How much energy would it take to send a beam of light 100 feet—the distance needed, Kingsborough believed, to make the game a truly long-range version of tag—and what was the best way of emitting that light? What WOW finally realized, after months of research which included studying real lasers, was that the secret would be in the target sensor. The more sensitive you could make it, the less powerful the beam of light had to be.

Focusing on the sensor also eliminated a second problem: How would you play the game outdoors? The sun emits infrared light and only a powerful sensor would be able to distinguish between a sunbeam and a Lazer Tag beam. Could you build a sensor that would be powerful enough? After months of effort, Kingsborough and staff had a prototype that took care of the problem. In fact, they could create every feature Rago had dreamed of as he sat around the pool, with one exception.

"We originally envisioned that you would see the beam of light—even in daylight—when you shot. But there was just no way to do it," Kingsborough says. "But we could do everything else. We could give kids something they always wanted to do. They wanted to tag someone 100 feet away, they wanted to be part of *Star Wars,* and now they could."

But the question still remained who would be playing with this creation? It was here that Kingsborough's understanding of what was going on in the toy industry came to the fore. Instead of trying to sell the game as a high tech version of tag to six, seven and eight year olds —the folks most likely to be seen running through the neighborhood yelling "You're it"—he aimed Lazer Tag at teenagers.

It was a different and decidedly risky approach. With the exception of sporting equipment (bats, balls, bikes) and some kinds of consumer electronics (computer games, brightly colored Walkmen and the like), virtually no toys are marketed to teenagers. The reason is simple. Besides being perhaps the most fickle human beings God ever put on Earth (just ask the parent who owns one), teenagers want above all else to appear grown-up. Babies play with toys; adults don't, goes their thinking, and no image-conscious teenager worth his Reeboks and Jams is going to play a kids' game. Still, Kingsborough thought marketing to teens might be worth the gamble.

"There were two issues," he explains. "Clearly we see marketing to older kids as a way of reaching younger ones. They see what the big kids are doing, and since they want to act older, they want to do it too. So that was one of our primary motives. The other was that we saw this teenage marketplace as being undermarketed. We said there is a good chance that teenagers want a product like this, so let's go ahead and give it to them."

But Kingsborough, the father of three—including two

teenagers—knew he couldn't position Lazer Tag as just a fancy game of tag. Teenagers would consider that totally uncool. So, from the very beginning, Lazer Tag was sold as a futuristic sport. The story behind it was that a thousand years from now there would be no war. All conflicts would be solved by nations playing Lazer Tag.

The idea was admittedly hokey, but it did effectively underscore the marketing message that this product was something more than a simple game of tag. And no matter how contrived the story line, the technology more than made up for it.

The prime component of Lazer Tag is the StarLyte, which sends out an infrared beam of light up to 100 feet. Players use the StarLyte to "tag" their opponent with the beam. They do that by having the light strike the StarSensor, an electro-optical device worn by all players. When the light hits the sensor, it emits an electronic tone and one of the score-keeping lights on the sensors is switched on. When you are tagged for a sixth time, a siren similar to the kind sounded by European police cars wails, and the game is over.

All of this was explained in a breathless press release, which even included a copy of a newspaper story written 1,000 years from now, heralding the product's arrival:

Luna City, The Moon (July 20, 3010)—The U.S. Lazer Tag Team scored an overwhelming victory over the favored Luna City Lazer Tag Team, beating them soundly in three games out of four. U.S. Team Captain Henderson attributed the win to the team's long experience in playing the game. Most of the players have competed in Lazer Tag tournaments since they were children. . . .

Freemont, Calif.—Take the classic game of tag, add the sleekness and sophistication of high technology and the fast action of a space adventure and you've got the exciting new-age game of tomorrow—Lazer Tag.

Lazer Tag is the first home tag game of its kind to combine state-of-the-art technology with a schoolyard classic to create a physical, highly interactive variation of the age-old children's game of tag. Lazer Tag creates a new toy category revolutionizing children's games. . . .

And as we have seen, publicity, hyperbolic or otherwise, is vital in Kingsborough's formula for creating new products.

"Great product is the first thing you have to have," he says. "If you have a poor product, the consumer will find out quickly and it will die fast. We either take technology and make a great product, or use the technology to improve an existing product. Either way, you can differentiate what you have when you promote it."

And public relations is the first part of that promotion effort. "You have to do great public relations, because word of mouth is still the best form of advertising there is. P.R. is the most credible way to get product sold." That is true because an effective public relations campaign gets people talking about your product. And people give much more credibility to what their neighbors tell them about an item, than they do to an ad.[1]

---

1. The remarkable success of Cabbage Patch dolls is the best example of that in the toy industry. While Coleco would go on to spend millions to advertise the homely dolls, the initial success of the dolls a few years back is directly attributable to a $500,000 public relations campaign which succeeded in, among other things, arranging for Nancy Reagan to give Cabbage Patch dolls

That public relations effort took two forms. Kingsborough and his senior staff gave scores of interviews, to every publication from the trade press to financial magazines, explaining what Lazer Tag was and why it would be a winner. "The problem with public relations is you can't be real analytical about it," Kingsborough explains. "You can't say I spent this much time doing interviews, and I got this many sales. You have to believe in it and you also—and this is real hard for senior management—have to spend the time and energy on it."

That's hard for many executives because most large companies—and WOW is no exception—have a public relations staff. Often executives, especially those who are uncomfortable with reporters, feel that their time would be better spent doing their own jobs instead of talking to the press. That's what the P.R. department is for, they say.

But as a rule, reporters—especially those for national publications—would much rather talk to a company's senior manager than to a public relations person. They want to get the information first hand.

Kingsborough decided from the start to make a reporter's life as simple as possible. Like many companies, WOW uses an outside public relations firm to supplement its internal effort. But unlike most firms, a senior executive of WOW's outside agency, Smith Marketing, has an office in WOW's headquarters; an office just down the hall from Kingsborough's. That not only makes it easier for the outside P.R. firm to know what is going on

---

to the children of Cambodian refugees—an event that was recorded by all three television networks and most newspapers.

inside the company and thereby easier to generate publicity, but it also makes it simple for them to locate Kingsborough should a reporter call. "You have to commit the time to public relations," Kingsborough says. "And you have to do it well."

The second part of the public relations effort called for attracting the attention of college students. "If college kids play Lazer Tag," Kingsborough says, "then it must be real cool."

To get them, WOW signed celebrities—everyone from pro athletes like Kareem Abdul-Jabbar and Olympic gold medal winner Greg Louganis to rock stars like the Bangles—to stage Lazer Tag demonstrations for the media. Some of WOW's staff toured college campuses, explaining the game and also explaining that the company would sponsor a collegiate Lazer Tag championship to determine which schools had the best shooters.

The strategy worked. By the time Lazer Tag started appearing in stores that fall, young people knew what it was. It became the best selling toy of 1986—even though it cost $39.95 for one StarLyte gun and $19.95 for one sensor. Since it takes at least two people to play, that meant the minimum you had to spend—not including buying the StarVest or StarHelmet—was $119.80. (Batteries and tax not included.)

Society has changed

What made Kingsborough even dream that a toy costing more than $100 would ever catch on?

"It is simple," he says. "Society has changed and the relationship between the parent and child has changed.

"Children go to school earlier, typically at age two as opposed to age five. Wives work, or have other interests that result in them spending less time with their children than they would like, and I guarantee that one of the important things to your child is another child. That is a big change. In my generation, family was the most important thing.

"There has also been a material change in society and so parents are more apt to gain approval by providing what the child wants, instead of making that decision for the child. Part of that comes from guilt. If you are spending less time with your child, you want to try to compensate, and one of the ways of doing that is by providing things, especially things they ask for."

Now, of course, not every parent is doing that and certainly no one is doing that all the time. But it does appear to even casual observers that more of this is going on than ever before. Maybe it is guilt. Maybe it is an attempt by parents to impress others by having their children wear $50 sneakers and play with $70 teddy bears. Whatever the reason, Kingsborough is right. More than ever before, parents are buying what kids want as opposed to making decisions about what the child should have.

"And when the child says the three magic words, 'I want one,' they are more likely to buy that specific product. The child is more likely to specify a particular item, because brand identification is much greater. Children see more advertising than ever before and they are more brand-aware because other kids tell them. Other kids say, 'I have a Teddy Ruxpin. Do you?' "

And while it's true that kids have always asked that

question about some item or other, Kingsborough says it gets asked earlier today. "It used to happen at age five, when they went to kindergarten. Now it happens at age two, when they go to preschool. It also happens because they have been exposed to more, they are more aware. You take your kid to Disney World. Did your parents take you as many places? No. We are a mobile society, today. Did you have color TV? They never knew it didn't exist. Kids experience more today at an earlier age than their parents, or even their older siblings did."

That is certainly true and with all this experience and exposure comes the unalterable fact that today's children —raised on color television, MTV and *USA Today*—will become bored more quickly. If Worlds of Wonder was going to design toys for these youngsters, relying heavily on technology to hold their interest, it would, by definition, be forced to sell expensive toys. Technology does not come cheap. But with the exception of bicycles, toys were selling for under $50, less than half of what it costs to play Lazer Tag. Kingsborough's new way of looking at the toy industry would force parents, and retailers, to rethink what a toy should cost.

"That was a potential problem," Kingsborough says, understating his challenge. "Retailers said it had to sell for $39 or $49. But it is my belief that price is only relative to other choices. If someone will pay $50 for a pair of Reebok shoes, why wouldn't they pay $60 or $70 for a teddy bear. The kid outgrows the Reeboks in four or five months. Selling Lazer Tag was made a little easier by products that had come before. Teddy Ruxpin and Cabbage Patch had each sold for more than $49, so that lessened some of retailers' reluctance.

"But people have changed," Kingsborough adds in explaining why he feels confident that his company can sell expensive toys, both now and in the future.

"The relative point of what is expensive has changed. Is $10 expensive? It used to be. Not any more. Ten- or twenty-dollar items are now spontaneous purchases. Here is a truism, but one people don't think of. Look in your wallet. Whatever is the highest bill is what you spend for a spontaneous purchase. For most people it is a twenty-dollar bill, and that is the amount you will spend on a spontaneous purchase. At least that. Ten years ago it would have been a five or a ten. I have a five-year-old. For him, it may be fifty dollars.

"Price is not an issue anymore. My parents wanted to buy me things that were basic and inexpensive—blocks, roller skates, guns. But there has been a basic change in America. America is not into inexpensive. It is into quality."

Notice what Kingsborough is saying. As long as there have been retailers, marketers have known there was a small segment of consumers who demanded the highest quality in what they bought and who would buy products that met their standards, no matter what the cost. But that isn't the market Kingsborough is after. He assumes he will get those people automatically. What he believes is that there is now a *huge* part of the market for whom price no longer matters. Maybe it should. Maybe, economists would argue, families with incomes under $35,000 shouldn't be spending $120 or $150 on Lazer Tag and its accessories. But the fact is, they are—and are doing so in huge numbers. These are the people Kingsborough is courting and he says he always knew they were there.

"When you were growing up, your father was more serious minded than you are. That has to do with how difficult it was to grow up when he did, and what he went through. You are part of the 'me' generation and the kids today are even more of the 'me' generation. In part, kids haven't changed. They have things in common with the kids who came before them, things that will remain common through all eternity. The social aspects of how kids are remain the same. They need other kids, because they don't want to be alone. They want to have group activities, and they want to learn.

"But it is also true that kids really have changed. They are more multidimensional and they have more interests. They go to school at an earlier age. They communicate more because there are more ways to communicate. They have telephones, portable telephones, television, VCRs, CDs. Did you have an answering machine when you were growing up? I guarantee your child will own one at some point.

"They are also more mobile. They spend more time away from their parents than any other generation, so they become more independent. They have changed in a lot of ways."

How do you know that this change has occurred? According to Kingsborough, it comes in part from reading a lot of research material during 15 years in the toy business, and part of it comes by trying to find patterns in the things he has observed.

But most of all, it comes from talking to kids and watching their reactions when he tests new ideas like Lazer Tag.

"The reason Worlds of Wonder can be successful is that

we say Let's find out what kids want," Kingsborough explains. "Let's do enough research to know what they want and then by understanding that, we'll know what it will take to get them to buy it, because it won't be us developing the toy in a vacuum. They've said they want it, all we are doing is giving it to them."

That idea isn't new, of course. What is different is that the concepts WOW chooses to test are always selected because they fit with Kingsborough's templet of what it takes to create a successful toy.

"It becomes very simple. You say this is what they want. This is the technology available. Now let's go find a product."

Not only does that make the process of creating a new toy easier, it also makes it much faster.

"At other toy companies, product development typically takes a couple of years," Kingsborough says. "We do it in six to nine months, because what we do is so well defined. Kids say they want a flying machine. There is the technology available that allows you to build one, and zap! There is the flying machine that kids expect."

What Kingsborough is saying is what good marketers have said since the beginning of time: To succeed, listen to your customer. But he is taking that a step further. Kingsborough is listening selectively, balancing what the customer says he wants, against what he believes gives Worlds of Wonder a competitive advantage. Having defined WOW as a company that translates existing technology, Kingsborough doesn't listen when the customer (i.e., the child) says he wants a different kind of molded-plastic toy. Sure, he can produce the toy, but it won't be one where WOW has an edge. Any toy company can produce a plastic toy. But let a seven year old say he wants to be Luke Skywalker, and Kingsborough pays attention. Those are the customers he wants. Knowing which customer to listen to is Kingsborough's first step in "never losing sight of the marketplace."

"The first thing you have to do is find out who ultimately buys your product, and find out what they want. Second, you find out who retails it, and ask them what they want. And finally you go to the inventors and you tell them what the other two have said.

"The source of the idea is not important," adds Kingsborough, who licensed Teddy Ruxpin from Alchemy II and developed Lazer Tag internally at WOW's offices in Fremont, California, just outside of San Jose. "It is the selection and implementation of good ideas that's important. You cannot hire enough people so that you have all the good ideas. I think that is what went on at Atari and I think it is a bad concept. I think the right concept is to figure out who has the best ideas and figure out what you do best. You concentrate on that, and if someone else has a good idea, buy it and make it successful."

Just tell me what you want

It all sounds fine. But you have to know what a good idea is. Kingsborough says kids will tell you. But can they?

Children are cute, clever, but usually not articulate about abstract concepts such as describing what would make the ideal toy. When you are dealing with small children—and as WOW has diversified, it now sells products geared to children as young as two years old—how do you find out what they really want?

"You don't ask them, you give them options and let them choose," says Kingsborough, whose office is filled with toys—everything from Teddy Ruxpin prototypes to rocking horses. "Generally, when you are testing what kids are oriented to, you get a broad category of products that have already been established—dolls, games, puzzles, you include everything—and you put a bunch of kids in a room and tell them they can pick only two. You'd be surprised about the number of kids the same age who pick the same toy. That tells what the orientation is."

That gives Kingsborough his starting point, and remember, he only wants to create toys that kids are predisposed to like.

The process relies almost strictly on emotion, and that is by design. "Most purchases have emotion in them," Kingsborough says "and purchases, especially in entertainment businesses, like toys, are almost all emotion. They are not analytical. What kids say is pretty up-front. They haven't learned to be calculating yet. So when they tell you things—'This is cool; that stinks'—we believe them. It is simply that.

"That is one of the things that differentiates us from other toy companies. They take what the kids say and have adults analyze it from the adult's point of view.

"I had to laugh. Recently, we had a real sophisticated outside group come in and they analyzed everything about what went on in a focus group. Then they gave me a detailed report on what the kids had said. I listened and then threw it in the garbage. They were analyzing it from a 40 year old's perspective, and I am not selling to 40 year olds! I want to know what kids think. I can analyze what a 40 year old thinks; I'm 40. But I am not 11, and I can't recreate being 11. The only one who knows how an 11 year old thinks is an 11 year old."

Given this approach to market research, you might think that when he was developing a new product like Lazer Tag, only the first ten seconds of a focus group would be important. It's in those few seconds that the kid says "I love it," or "I hate it." You might think that, but Kingsborough says you'd be wrong.

"You need the whole thing," he says. "but what you are alluding to is something different. You don't want the influence of outside forces where the person running the focus group can influence what goes on. That's true.

"But you want the whole thing. You want to know what the child says initially. Then you want to give them a chance to play with it, to see what they think, and then you want to give them alternatives, to see what they think of them. You need all those parts, but you don't need any guiding. That is why we videotape most of our focus groups so I can actually see the process in addition to the reports.

"That's the other thing. When I was consulting, I saw the problem caused by delegation. You can delegate the gathering of information, and you can delegate the creation of processes, but you can't delegate experience and intuitiveness. Those things are the reason you are in a senior position, yet I see people delegating things where experience is vitally important. That is the wrong thing to delegate. You are where you are because of everything you are. Not because of part of what you are. And you must stay involved. You can't run a toy company by looking at computer printouts of the numbers."

That strategy is one that would seem to combat the Peter Principle, the name for the not-so-facetious syndrome which states that people are promoted to the level at which they become incompetent. If the principle is true—and if you think about the last time you had to deal with a large organization, you'll realize it is—what Kingsborough is suggesting makes sense. There is a reason people are promoted. Instead of ignoring the skills that moved them up a rung on the corporate ladder, you should take advantage of them.

That is what Kingsborough did with Lazer Tag. He personally reviewed the videotaped focus groups that were part of Lazer Tag's development. Not surprisingly, what struck him were the emotions of the kids who played with it. "The minute we handed it to them, they'd smile. When we talked to them, they absolutely knew what it was and they knew how to play with it. Any time you have to give people instructions that take an hour to figure out, it is a tough product to sell. And after they played with it, they still liked it."

Kingsborough, who knew Lazer Tag would be a hit once Rago explained the concept to him, had just gotten market confirmation he was right. Now it was just a matter of building the products and designing the advertising. In the Worlds of Wonder scheme of things, neither is completely set until just before a game is shipped.

"After an idea is born, it is constantly being changed and refined. I think this is a real big advantage. People make point-in-time decisions, but it still takes at least six months from the point they make that decision to get the product to market. In that time, society has changed somewhat, people's needs have changed, technology has changed. You need to audit your decisions and refine them, to adjust to the changes."

But you can't change too much. More than half of the toys sold in this country are purchased between September and December. And for that holiday push, retailers buy early in the year. Typically they write orders at the toy shows held during the first quarter. If a buyer decides he wants 5,000 dozen green whosits at the New York Toy Fair in February, and you—because you want to keep refining your product—keep fiddling until you have a red whatsit come September, you will not have happy retailers.

"Our changes are never 180 degrees," Kingsborough says. "They are generally 20 degrees, 30 degrees. But it is generally that last fine tuning that really does make the difference. I'll give you an example. Teddy Ruxpin, all the way up until we finished engineering, was a skinnier bear with large eyes. That changed just before we went in production. He became a little plumper. His face is a little fuller. He isn't bug-eyed. We think it makes it a much cuter bear.

"We go through that process on everything, and the reason isn't any different than the reasons for everything else we do. As you learn more about something, you become more focused on it and you are able to make more intelligent decisions."

With Lazer Tag, what kept changing during the development process was the shape of the StarLyte. From the outset, Kingsborough had decided it shouldn't look like a gun. "We thought it should be like the phasers [guns] used on 'Star Trek,' and look like a garage-door opener." The problem with that, WOW discovered when they had children test the prototype of the rectangular StarLyte, was there was no good way to aim the device. They'd constantly shoot and miss. "If you couldn't hit your target, it wouldn't be any fun." A sight was added and the more the engineers fiddled with the shape of the Star-Lyte, the more gunlike it became.[2]

Not surprisingly, when Lazer Tag was introduced at the New York Toy Fair in February 1986, critics charged that WOW was promoting violence, a charge that Kingsborough says simply isn't true. "Originally we thought of it as a game like tag, we never really intended it to be a war toy."

Now, the toy industry is criticized all the time. Parents' groups frequently object to "war toys," and in recent years, consumer groups have complained that Saturday-morning cartoon shows are really nothing more than 30-, 60- and 90-minute commercials for the toys featured on the program.[3] So the complaints were to be expected.

More troublesome, though, was the allegation that,

2. Perhaps too much so. In April 1987, Leonard Falcon, age 19, and three of his friends were playing Lazer Tag near the Central Elementary School in Rancho Cucamonga, California, about 45 miles east of Los Angeles. According to *Time* magazine, here is what happened:

During the mock combat, Falcon jumped from behind bushes, assumed a shooting stance and fired his plastic pistol at an obscure figure. In the next instant Falcon was killed, after two shotgun blasts were fired by a sheriff's deputy.

Authorities say the officer was investigating a report of armed prowlers in the schoolyard; in the darkness the distinct flash of light from the toy gun made it look as if a real pistol were being fired. . . .

3. And it does seem that way. Most of the television shows on Saturday morning do have a product tie-in. If your child is watching 90 minutes of "Smurfs" on Saturday morning, isn't he more likely to want a Smurf doll? The toy companies, including Worlds of Wonder, apparently think so. Developing a television program to accompany the introduction of a new toy is now standard operating procedure in the industry.

with Lazer Tag, and indeed with almost all of WOW's products, Kingsborough is robbing children of their imagination. Playing regular tag, critics say, allows kids to imagine infinite variations. As they run after someone they can be anyone from Superman to their favorite sports hero; from cowboys to Indians. Lazer Tag just gave them one choice: They are simply a character out of a *Star Wars*-like movie.

Not surprisingly, Kingsborough quickly dismisses the critics.

"I think the people who say that have not seen kids play with our toys. To say that we inhibit the imagination is simply wrong. I think anything that brings what you imagine closer to reality expands your imagination."

Going for the gold

Indeed, that was the purpose of the Lazer Tag advertising produced by Chiat/Day. Set somewhere in the future —when all conflict was resolved by playing the game— teenagers and young adults were shown in a stadium playing Lazer Tag, while thousands looked on and cheered. "We wanted to convey in the advertising something they had already planted in their heads," Kingsborough says. "They had seen *Star Trek*, and *Star Wars* and *Battlestar Galactica,* so we set about creating an advertising campaign that would leave you with the idea that you had just seen one of them."

And he spent as much time helping to create the advertising as he did designing the product and orchestrating the public relations campaign.

Kingsborough, who believes in breaking down ideas

into their separate components, ticks off the three things he believes lead to great advertising.

"First is the concept. We spent enormous amounts of time on the concept. But most companies do that, so I don't think we are different there. But I think we are different in that developing the concept is a senior-management responsibility, not a junior-management responsibility." Again, that goes to Kingsborough's point that senior managers have earned their position for a reason and it would be silly not to take advantage of their expertise.

"Second, we spend a lot of time on the production side of advertising, and that is a place where a lot of companies start dropping the ball. They buy off on the concept, and they leave production to the ad agency. We don't do that.

"Finally, and this is where literally all the companies drop the ball, we want to be as smart with the buy [where and when the commercial will appear] as we were with the concept.

"Where is the best buy? What is the best way to spend your money? You are going to spend $500,000 developing the commercial, but you are going to spend $10 million on running it. Why not be as smart on that end as you are on the front end? Here, we are real different. We spend an awful lot of time on it, instead of leaving it to the agency."

With Lazer Tag, that meant focusing on the teenage— particularly *male* teenage—market. Lazer Tag spots ran on MTV, and were also featured prominently during NCAA championship games. The message: This is a high tech sport.

The ads got the message across. In the first commercial, players wearing futuristic hairdos are always photographed in electric-blue light. Dressed in what look like spacesuits, they enter a crowded stadium filled with a cheering crowd. The game begins and soon players are diving left and right and soaring over opponents, all the while shooting their StarLytes. At the end, an announcer —whose voice would be perfect for announcing the end of the world—says: "Lazer Tag, the game that moves at the speed of light."

Then, to prove that WOW has some perspective on all this, he adds, "from Worlds of Wonder; stadium not included."

While there was another attempt at humor (one execution was a James Bond takeoff, where a 007-like character is summoned by M to preview his government's latest weapon: a StarLyte, of course), most played on the futuristic theme. In the best-known spot, the American and Russian teams play in the 310th Annual Statue of Liberty Challenge, an event the Americans have won for 74 years straight. And while it appears at the outset that the Russians will finally win, the Americans stage an "unbelievable comeback" (as the breathless announcer tells us) and are heading toward certain victory as the commercial ends. The tag line: "Practice hard America."

America was eager to do just that. By the time Lazer Tag began turning up in stores in August 1986, Americans were primed to buy and they rushed to seek out the Lazer Tag displays at toy, department and discount stores. "And that is the last thing you have to do," Kingsborough says. "You have to do great point-of-purchase [the display that appears in the store]. That is where you tie together everything you have done before.

"When someone walks into that store, they should say, 'I read about it, and saw the commercial, now let me take a look at this thing.' Right then is where the display has got to initiate the purchase. It has to say *buy me*."

It apparently did. WOW's success with Teddy Ruxpin, coupled with its aggressive advertising and public relations campaign, convinced retailers to give Lazer Tag prominent display, often at the beginning or the end of the aisle. It was not uncommon to see boxes stacked ten high by ten wide on the shelves.

The black-gray-and-red packaging reinforced the television commercials. The toy's logo, which features L-A-Z-E-R T-A-G in futuristic lettering and had appeared at the end of each commercial, was set in large type on the box. And the graphics made it appear that you would be buying a product that came from a new civilization.

"We knew Lazer Tag was going to do very well," Kingsborough says. "The question was would it be number 1, or 20 [in the ranking of toy sales for 1986]. We knew we had a win."

It turned out to be a substantial one. Worlds of Wonder shipped more than 2.5 million units, recording well in excess of $100 million in revenue.

The size may have been surprising but, Kingsborough says, the success wasn't.

"There are four things you have to do in creating a success: First, take technology and make a great product, one that enhances the basic play value in some way that kids know about, or have dreamed about. Then you do great public relations. Then great advertising. And finally you do great point-of-purchase.

"If you do those four things, you will sell a lot of product. We did and we were.

"It wasn't just happenstance; the strategy works."

Once up and running, Kingsborough has worked hard to maintain his lead, understanding the fickle nature of toy buyers. (When was the last time you stood in line to buy a Pac Man video game or Cabbage Patch doll?) To prolong Lazer Tag's life, he added new products: There is now a StarLyte Pro that shoots 300 feet. And if you are going to aim at things that far away, you may want to let your teammate know what you are up to so there are now Lazer Tag walkie talkies. All of this is consistent with the templet, which calls for cutting off the competition. There is even a Saturday morning cartoon show, *Lazer Tag Academy*.[4]

---

4. We quote from WOW's description of the show:

Welcome to the year 3010. Lazer Tag is the international sport. Each year, grand Lazer Tag championship games are held across a variety of age groups. The Lazer Tag Academy, a prestigious international foundation, is devoted to the continued peace, prosperity and advancement of mankind.

Jamie Jaren is a bright, friendly thirteen-year-old girl and three-time winner of the Trans-Global Lazer Tag Championships. Jamie is the star pupil of professor Nori Olanga, head of the StarLyte Academy.

Professor Olanga has discovered that Jamie possesses a curious power over the energy emitted from the Lazer Tag StarLyte unit. Jamie can use StarLyte energy to manipulate the physical world as well as travel through time.

But then Draxon Drear arrives, a master criminal from the past. Drear plans to change the world into an evil place and he, too, has power over StarLyte energy. The only person who can thwart Drear's evil plan is Jamie Jaren.

Drear decides to travel to the year 1987 to kidnap Jamie's ancestor,

Producing the number-one-selling toy in your first two years of existence is no mean trick. It is also something that could not last forever. Kingsborough expected to be dethroned—if only temporarily—by others in the industry. "There are other smart people out there," he said to a visitor while he was riding high. But internal problems caused his fall.

Although Teddy Ruxpin and Lazer Tag ensured Worlds of Wonder's place in the history of the toy business, the company would be increasingly plagued with rising costs and manufacturing and delivery problems. The result: The company filed for bankruptcy protection in late 1987.

The filing ironically underscored Kingsborough's templet for success. His first point, the need to do "great product," remains true. But as Worlds of Wonder's woes reveal, producing great product goes beyond mere technical excellence.

Tom Jaren. Tom is a fourteen-year-old athletic boy living in Los Angeles. Drear reasons that by changing history, Jamie Jaren will never be born and no one will be able to stop Drear.

Jamie discovers this evil plot and she, too, travels to 1987 to protect her relatives: Tom, her sister Beth and his brother Nicky Jaren.

Join Jamie, Tom, Beth and Nicky on Saturdays on NBC as they travel through time to stop the villain Draxon Drear. Every Saturday you'll see a new adventure and learn more about the game of the future. Who knows? Maybe you possess special power over StarLyte energy, too.

"Hi ho Silver":
5 Selling to a crowd of nonbuyers

Managers from Southwestern Bell Publications, the division of the phone company that assembles and prints directories, were bored. They had spent more than eight hours in the air, on the plane ride from their headquarters in St. Louis to Maui where they would hold their sales meeting, and that didn't include the delays. First, the plane was late. Then they had to wait for their luggage, and finally the buses that would take them to their hotel didn't show up. But things picked up once their three-bus caravan finally got underway and headed toward their hotel.

About ten minutes into the ride, the people in the lead bus watched as the bus that had been following them suddenly zoomed past.

"We can't let them beat us," someone called out from the back.

"That's right," came the response from up front. And suddenly everyone on board began yelling "Faster, faster. Catch 'em."

"I can't break the speed limit," the driver said to the group of mainlanders he thought had suddenly lost their senses.

"There's ten bucks in it for you if we arrive at the hotel first," came the reply.

RON JENNINGS of Southwestern Bell Publications

With that, he floored the accelerator, and retook the lead. As they arrived first at the hotel, someone handed the driver ten dollars and the Southwestern Bell's senior staff left the bus and entered the hotel cheering, much to the confusion of the hotel staff.

"That's what this group is all about," says one of the members of the winning bus. "We are full of fun, and competitive as hell." That explanation goes a long way toward revealing why a utility company ended up being included on the list of the best marketing companies in America. Making the list baffles Ron Jennings, at first.

Jennings, 46, is a salesman, and one of the old school at that. His clothes are impeccable, and his voice booms, even when he orders a hamburger "with more than my fair share of french fries." And the order is accompanied with a couple of suggestions that are enough to make the 19-year-old waitress shake her head as she walks toward the kitchen. But even Jennings isn't brash enough to suggest Southwestern Bell should be called a marketing star.

But clearly it is. Though Southwestern Bell didn't even have a marketing department until 1978, Jennings and his staff identified a market that is still untapped by most companies. They've created a product in a mature area of publishing that nevertheless has the potential of doing $500 million in revenues a year, forever. To put that in perspective, $500 million in sales would safely place a freestanding company on the *Fortune* 500.

And they did this *with a phone book;* one designed for senior citizens at that.

It was accomplished with simple, straightforward salesmanship.

Within the first 15 minutes on the job, a new salesman is told "you are not selling a product, you are selling a solution to a customer's problem. And that's true, even though the customer may not know he has a problem." And that's how Jennings approached his task.

Selling another phone book as just another phone book would have been virtually impossible. Who needs another phone book? But Jennings turned the proposition around. "Suppose," he asked potential advertisers, "I could show you a way to increase your business [your problem], and tap into a huge market with lots of money [the solution to the problem]. Would you be interested?"

Questions like these are likely to get your foot in the door.

But, although the approach is classic, it was one that would have been impossible prior to the breakup of AT&T.

Back then, Southwestern Bell Publications put out the phone books for virtually every town in the five states of the old Bell system it served—Texas, Oklahoma, Missouri, Kansas and Arkansas—and almost nobody else did. Oh, there might be an occasional enterpreneur who would publish a Yellow Pages (the term had never been protected by AT&T) for a ten-block area in Houston, but that was rare.

The only companies with the resources to seriously challenge Southwestern Bell ("Taco Bell," to the rest of the AT&T system) would have been the other regional Bell companies, but that was unthinkable. Prior to divestiture, there was a gentleman's agreement among the AT&T subsidiaries not to move into each other's territory. "We didn't mess with each other," is the way one top executive put it. There was little to be gained by doing so.

Consider what would have happened if prior to divestiture New Jersey Bell had decided that it wanted to sell phone books in Kansas City. New Jersey Bell would gain some business, and Southwestern Bell would lose some, but the total amount of money earned—all of which was going to AT&T at the time—would remain the same.

Besides, moving into a new territory meant dealing with new public-utility commissions and the only thing worse than competition was facing a new set of regulators. Speaking for the rest of the AT&T system, one executive summed up the problem this way: "You can't win with utility commissions. If we had been successful in taking on someone else within the Bell system, the regulators would have said we should have been and they would have used the additional earnings to lower our charges elsewhere. If we failed, they'd say, 'That's your problem,' and would have made us eat the loss."

No wonder there was no competition and no wonder a marketing department was an afterthought.

All that changed on January 1, 1984, the day Ma Bell died at the hands of the federal government. As part of its agreement with the Justice Department, which thought having one dominant phone company was anticompetitive, AT&T was freed to enter new business. In exchange, the phone company agreed to shed its local operating companies, such as Southwestern Bell. It happened in two steps: First, AT&T's twenty-two local subsidiaries were combined into seven regional Bell operating companies (RBOCs)—Pacific Telesis and U.S. West in the western part of the country; Southwestern

Bell and Ameritech in middle America; and BellSouth, Bell Atlantic and Nynex along the East Coast.

Then, the RBOCs were spun off into freestanding public companies able to compete wherever and however they wanted to, subject only to a few restrictions that governed the breakup of AT&T. Each RBOC began operating cellular-telephone networks—indeed, in 1986 Southwestern Bell would pay more than $1 billion to buy Metromedia's car-phone business—but most also rushed off to enter new fields.

Computers, real estate or phone books?

Pacific Telesis, headquartered in San Francisco, bought Byte Shops, a computer retailing chain, and Kensington Datacom, a private data network. Colorado-based U.S. West acquired Commercial Funding, a financial-services company, and started a real estate development and management firm. Ameritech, headquartered in Chicago, bought Applied Data Research, a software supplier, and acquired a stake in a company that made computer work stations. And what was Southwestern Bell doing while its former sister companies were moving into high tech and high finance? It was deciding to publish more phone books.

To be sure, during predivestiture planning, Southwestern Bell officials had more exciting things in mind. For a while, the company was convinced it would move into airplane leasing and travel services. Given the thousands of square miles in its service territory, the move seemed to make sense.

But every time the company did projections showing

the return on its investment in the travel business—or anything else—it kept coming to the same conclusion: There was nothing more profitable than publishing phone books. Says almost everyone you talk to at Southwestern Bell, "We decided to stick to our knitting." Indeed, the company adopted the advertising slogan, "Making the most of what we do best." It may not be a great line, but the philosophy behind it certainly is, and sticking to it took more discipline than many senior managers have.

In an attempt to leave their mark, executives who suddenly find themselves in charge of successful, but boring, companies often try to change the existing order. And publishing phone books is nothing if not boring. The first phone book (with 21 listings) came off the presses in 1877, just a year after Alexander Graham Bell invented the telephone, and most hard-charging managers would find little excitement in doing something that has been done for more than 100 years.

And there would have been a tangible incentive for doing something new. An announcement that Southwestern Bell was moving into gene splicing or some other sexy field would have helped the company's image on Wall Street. There, too, new is always better—at least initially. Given the company's decision to concentrate on publishing directories, the price of its stock trailed those of the other "Baby Bells," as the RBOCs quickly became known.

The reaction of the investment community to Southwestern Bell's decision to do more of the same was summed up in a drawing *Forbes* used to illustrate an article about the Baby Bells. While the other regional phone companies were shown as gunslingers and race-car drivers, *Forbes* used a picture of an old Ma Bell sitting on the porch in a rocking chair to characterize Southwestern Bell. To this day, the illustration causes grumbling in the hallways of Southwestern Bell Publications' five-story glass building located along Route 270 in suburban St. Louis.

Still, as Jennings (who heads Southwestern Bell's phone book business) points out, every time the company reviewed its future, everyone started with the same assumption. "I don't think there was ever a time that we didn't think we would be publishing phone books."

In retrospect, given the company's success, it looks like a simple decision.

It wasn't.

First, the desire to dance to Wall Street's tune cannot be underestimated. If you want a quick example, look at what happened to the folks up the road in Chicago who make Velveeta and Philadelphia Cream Cheese. When Wall Street declared that mergers were the best way for a company to prosper, Kraft merged with Dart Drug to become Dart & Kraft. But just a few years later, smaller aggressive companies were the darlings of "The Street." Not surprisingly, all the talk about the "synergy" that was going to be created by combining Dart and Kraft was forgotten and the company was divided back into two parts.

But, besides being willing to risk the scorn of Wall Street and the sneers of the people at your country club —two major reasons, cynics could say, for most of the merger and acquisition activity in the early 1980s— there were more serious reasons to look quizzically at the decision of Southwestern Bell to keep concentrating on publishing directories.

As late as October 1983, just two months before it would become a freestanding company, Southwestern Bell's chief executive was referring to phone books as a "mature business." At a meeting of his senior staff that fall, Chairman Al C. Parsons said, almost in passing: "We must begin to develop new products and prepare for the day this traditional revenue stream [the Yellow Pages] dries up. Market demand is expected to start declining steadily within the next ten years."

There were three reasons for Parsons's pessimism, and two of them involved high tech. The thought of "electronic delivery systems" was all the rage in the early 1980s. Everybody from Knight-Ridder to garage tinkerers were experimenting with ways of delivering information via your television set. You would simply turn on the set, punch a couple of buttons on the computer keyboard located nearby and be able to learn about everything from the specials at K Mart, to the phone number for the florist on Main Street. When the day came that these kinds of systems were as common as VCRs—and the projections that Parsons was referring to said that would happen by the early 1990s—who would need a phone book?

Related to that worry were the "talking Yellow Pages," which had started to capture the imagination of the public. You'd call a general number, type in the code for a particular category—say, shoemakers—and a computerized voice would give you the names of several nearby cobblers.

And if electronics weren't about to kill the Yellow

Pages, there was a good chance that old age might. By 1983, Yellow Pages revenues had reached $6.2 billion and the "experts" were beginning to question how much more room there was to grow. Buying space in the Yellow Pages accounted for 4.6 percent of all money spent on advertising in 1975. A decade later, that figure was up to 5.7 percent and the consensus was that its share of the advertising pie wasn't going to get much bigger.

Still, when Southwestern Bell began planning for the future, it kept reaching the same conclusion. People had been sounding the death knell for directories for years— indeed, the technology that was supposed to put the Yellow Pages out of business is no closer to becoming a reality today than it was five years ago—and, boring though it may be, there was no better business.

The decision had two parts—financial and cultural— and each was equally important.

Printing money

The first thing to understand is that printing phone books can be amazingly profitable. Southwestern Bell averages 22 percent *net* margins on the books. That is triple what AT&T earns and more than *four times* the average profits reported by members of the *Fortune* 500.

It is easy to understand how this comes about. Because ink and paper are bought in huge quantities, material costs are low. Equipment—printing presses and the like —require huge outlays to begin with, but once they are in place there is little left to buy. That leaves labor as the biggest variable cost, and even here Southwestern Bell had a huge advantage.

Long before the Justice Department ever dreamed of breaking up the phone company, Southwestern Bell had moved to cut costs. Not because company officials thought they might be running an independent phone company someday—15 years ago, nobody thought that would happen—they did it because it made sense. With five separate divisions (the five states of its service territory), each producing its own phone books, it was easy to spot wasted effort. Each state made its own purchases, did its own design, and had its own manufacturing facilities.

So, starting in the early 1970s, Southwestern Bell began to standardize. Uniform systems that resulted in each directory being produced the same way were implemented and computer systems were installed.

The timing was perfect. Just as the company started to become more efficient, the regional economy—led by the oil producers in Texas and Oklahoma—took off. With the papers filled with stories of gold being pumped out of the ground, recession-weary workers in what the business press had started to call the "Rust Belt" flocked south. Thousands of stores sprang up to take care of their needs and almost every one of them advertised in the Southwestern Bell Yellow Pages. And each year it cost them more to do so.

As the economy started soaring, so did Southwestern Bell's advertising rates. The company's argument for rate hikes of 12 to 15 percent a year was simple: More people were using the books and if you are reaching a broader audience, you ought to pay more. (The unspoken argument to advertisers was: Your only choice is to pay the increases . . . or not advertise in the Yellow Pages.)

The result of all this? By the time divestiture came about, Southwestern Bell accounted for nearly 20 percent of the Bell system's Yellow Pages revenues, even though it only had 10 percent of the phone lines. Ad revenues, which had been $75 million in 1971, had gone up eightfold, to $600 million, by 1984.

This strong foundation built of low costs and high revenues was made even stronger by a quirk in the way divestiture worked. The process of combining the old 22 Bell subsidiaries into seven freestanding units meant that in every case—with one exception—two or more subsidiaries would have to be forged together. The exception: Southwestern Bell.

So while New Jersey Bell and Bell of Pennsylvania merged to create Bell Atlantic, and the handful of companies that had served the Rocky Mountain states were combined into U.S. West, Southwestern Bell became a freestanding entity without any additions or subtractions.

That gave Southwestern Bell a headstart when it came to publishing directories. It had already completed the difficult task of centralizing its publishing operation, something the other regionals would later be forced to go through, and that lead would turn out to be extremely important.

As they approached divestiture, Southwestern Bell officials learned through casual conversations that the other regional phone companies would also be trying to expand their directory operations, but it certainly wasn't going to be where they put all their energies following divestiture. Still, they had discovered that phone books were a very profitable business, and like Southwestern

Bell they feared that if they stood pat and just tried to publish books on their home turf, they'd be inviting competitors to come in and nibble away at their market.

But understanding that was not enough. The other regional phone companies still had to standardize their separate directory operations, something that Southwestern Bell had already done. And while they were getting organized, Taco Bell was up and running.

Having decided to concentrate on directories, Southwestern Bell started a systematic marketing effort, really for the first time. Up until this point, there had been little reason to worry about marketing. AT&T had handled all the national advertising, and competitors like MCI were still seen more as an annoyance than a threat.

But divestiture had changed all that. So, Southwestern Bell set out to compete in this strange, new environment. But remember, divestiture or no divestiture, this was still a utility company used to moving slowly and carefully. The first thing Southwestern Bell did was make absolutely sure that every part of its five-state territory had one of its phone books. Only then did it start expanding, and even there the approach was decidedly cautious. Instead of looking for new products to introduce, Southwestern Bell began searching for bases its competitors might have left uncovered.

For example, in the Baltimore–Washington area and in Pinellas County, Florida, the boundaries for existing phone books had been drawn by using the city or county limits. That may have made sense for politicians, but it had nothing to do with the way people shopped. For example, a Clearwater resident got a Clearwater directory that didn't include stores and services in nearby St. Petersburg. "The boundaries were set up in a noncompetitive environment," said Jennings, who has more than a passing resemblance to John Z. De Lorean. "Businesses and shoppers did not like it, and we felt there was enough advertiser unrest for us to produce a successful directory that would appeal to people who shopped beyond the city limits."

In New York, NYNEX was publishing its Yellow Pages in two separate editions, one designed to meet consumer needs, the other intended strictly for businesses. The decision was more than a little confusing. Let's say you needed to buy paper for your personal computer. Where were you supposed to look, in the business-to-business or the consumer Yellow Pages? After careful study, Southwestern Bell decided to publish a New York Yellow Pages that put the phone books back together again.

Again, the approach to each new region was slow and methodical, and the marketing questions Southwestern Bell asked were basic: In what new places can we offer our existing product? What obvious holes have our competitors left in their markets? Southwestern Bell's fundamental approach to marketing is understandable. They were new to all this. When asked about the kind of marketing innovations Southwestern Bell had introduced prior to divestiture, Jennings points to things like the decision to introduce red ink for some ads and the creation of different-sized display ads. Those are fine, but not exactly the sort of things that put you on the fast track at Pepsi. They are the kinds of incremental improvements you would expect from utility companies which often take years to study the potential impact a change in the way they do business may have.

But Ron Jennings just laughs when he's asked if the same care went into the creation of the Silver Pages, its directory targeted to seniors. "Hell no," he says with his booming bass voice. "Bob Pope read about it in a newspaper."

Fifty isn't fatal

Robert Pope, formerly vice president for strategic planning for Southwestern Bell, had become vice chairman of the publications division following divestiture. And like all good managers, he met periodically with top staff members like Jennings. "In February of 1984, and it really did happen just this way, I was doing a little rundown for him of what my folks were working on," Jennings recalls, trying to repress a smile. "In January we had put together a marketing group and we had started to look at different parts of the country where we might start publishing a directory. Pope listened, said it was wonderful, and then asked 'Are you working on anything for senior citizens?' "

"Should we be?" Jennings asked.

And then Pope started quoting from an article he had read the day before. It was a newspaper clipping that would end up radically changing the lives of the folks at Southwestern Bell. It was also an article that shows how much luck has to do with uncovering what turn out to be terrific marketing insights.

What Pope had seen in the *Wall Street Journal* was one of the first articles to deal with the startling information that would come out of the 1980 Census. Up until that time, most marketers believed that life—at least in terms of consumer spending—ended at 49. They viewed people 50 and older as making up a small, unappealing market that pinched every penny. Television was the best example of that. Not only were there very few stars 50 or over on network shows in the early 1980s, but the key audience the networks promised to deliver to advertisers were aged 18–49, with adults aged 18–34 being considered to be the prime prospects. Those were the people with money, according to the marketing gurus.

But the census data and subsequent work by researchers proved something that marketing stars have always known. Consumers change. The new numbers showed that people over 50 had become the fastest-growing segment of the population. But even more important than their numbers was their wealth. While people over 50 accounted for just 25 percent of the population, this long-neglected group owns half of the nation's disposable income.

It is easy to understand why. People 50 and over have completed, or are close to completing, the major expenses —mortgages, child-rearing and college costs—that younger folks are saddled with. And you can afford to buy more than a new shuffleboard set if you don't have to pay to put junior through college and write out four-figure mortgage checks each month.

Given all this, Pope wondered if it made sense for Southwestern Bell to develop a directory designed for older consumers.

Jennings wasn't sure. This was the first time he had given any serious thought to seniors, and he had no idea if the information in the *Wall Street Journal* was right. Even if it was, how could he take advantage of it? Yes, older Americans are a clear market segment, but they are a huge one—some 60 or so million people. What could they all have in common, and how could Southwestern Bell design a product to reach them?

But you don't rise from selling Yellow Pages advertising in Kansas City to becoming an executive vice president by ignoring the boss when he asks you a question. "I told him in 30 days I would know everything there was to know about the group," says Jennings. And with that promise, prompted more by a desire not to look dumb than anything else, the idea that would lead to the Silver Pages was underway.

After the meeting, Jennings gathered his top aides. "I told them I had just made a commitment to determine if a senior citizen directory would work." There was nothing unusual about that. Directory officials are always looking to publish specialty phone books. At the time, competitors had on the market everything from a Christian Yellow Pages to one for gays. So, the fact that Jennings wanted them to explore publishing one for seniors —a potentially lucrative idea if they could figure out a way to do it—was fine. Except for one thing: Nobody had any idea of where to begin. Then someone remembered seeing a decal on a nearby International House of Pancakes saying that the restaurant accepted a senior citizen discount card. Well, that was a start.

Eventually, Southwestern Bell discovered that the card came from the St. Louis chapter of the National Association of Area Agencies on Aging. The NAAAA was an outgrowth of the Older Americans Act, a 1965 piece of federal legislation which called for the creation of a formal network of public and private agencies to improve the life of older Americans. The NAAAA's more than 650 branches coordinate and provide funds for groups that provide services to the elderly.

Jennings met with the St. Louis area agency and discovered that they had a huge problem that he could easily solve. "One of the things they were trying to do was encourage area merchants to give seniors discounts, and their next logical step was trying to figure out a way to tell seniors the discounts were available," Jennings recalls. "They were in the middle of their second attempt to publish a directory. They figured they had about 165,000 seniors in the area, but only enough funding to produce 6,000 books."

The problem cried out for Southwestern Bell's help. Who, after all, was better equipped to publish directories? And if they were having trouble in St. Louis, then the situation was probably the same in Kansas City and Chicago and. . . .

But while there was large opportunity, there was an even larger problem. Seniors groups had been burned in the past by companies claiming to want to help them. Everyone from stockbrokers to real estate companies had promised they were going to help make the lives of seniors easier, only to end up cheating older people out of their money. This was going to be a very difficult market to reach, and by this point Jennings, who had confirmed the numbers in the *Wall Street Journal* article, knew he wanted to reach them. Seniors, he was convinced, were and would continue to be for the foreseeable future a terrific market. And terrific markets, that is groups with common characteristics and lots of disposable income, were more in demand than ever before.

With the growing diversity in consumers' lifestyles, mass marketing has become less efficient. That's true, in part, because mass-marketing techniques themselves are less efficient. In 1975, if you ran an ad on all three networks simultaneously, you would have reached 93 percent of everyone who was watching television at that moment. By 1985, that same ad would have been seen by fewer than three of every four viewers, thanks to the rise of cable and independent television stations.

But, more important, the market itself has fragmented. Once the best way to sell disposable diapers was to run an ad during the daytime soap operas. But with more than half of all mothers with young children in the workforce today, that no longer makes as much sense.

Given these changes, advertisers—at least the smart ones—are becoming more selective. Everyone is looking for areas of disproportionate affluence, and here seniors clearly lead the pack. They make up a market that controls more than $7 trillion of wealth.

The question for Jennings was how to reach them.

Win-win-win

Jennings faced two distinct problems. First, he would have to prove to seniors that he meant no harm. That, not surprisingly, put him at a large disadvantage in getting his message across. Most advertisers face a relatively neutral audience. Either the consumer has never heard of what they have, or they know about the kind of product the marketer is offering but they already have a brand preference. In either case, the consumer is likely to be skeptical, but not downright hostile.

But with his new directory, Jennings was facing a situation like the one reputable direct-mail marketers faced in the 1970s, when they tried to sell merchandise to people who had been burned in the past by companies that took their money, but never sent a package. Like the direct-mail customers of a decade before, seniors had good reason to question any company that was offering a product designed to help them.

The successful direct-mail marketers, such as L.L. Bean and Land's End, won consumers over by providing terrific customer service and by keeping their word—and Jennings would too. It was here that being a utility company, with its almost genetic predisposition to move slowly, proved to be a major help.

Jennings began by being honest. Yes, he said, he was out to make money for Southwestern Bell, but that didn't mean he had to exploit senior citizens to do it. Jennings proved that with a number of relatively simple moves. For example, he promised that the phone company would not sell whatever mailing lists it developed, making it much harder for businesses that prey on seniors to take advantage of what Southwestern Bell was doing. And he committed Southwestern Bell to becoming one of the foremost sponsors of events—like the senior Olympics—which portrayed people over 60 in a positive light.

But the bigger challenge was coming up with a reason why seniors should take the Silver Pages—as Southwestern Bell had decided to call the new directory—into their homes. Jennings would have to prove there was something in it for both seniors and their advocates, the area agencies on aging. Without that acceptance by the market he was trying to reach, he'd never be able to sell a single ad.

Jennings first concentrated on winning over the agencies. It was a clever decision. If he could convince them that the Silver Pages had merit, he would have a much better chance of selling the seniors themselves. An endorsement from the National Association of Area Agencies on Aging would go a long way toward lessening whatever skepticism seniors had.

"Somewhere in the spring, my staff got me a couple of meetings with the people in Washington," Jennings recalls. "It meant a great deal to have the name Southwestern Bell behind us. These groups get presentations every day from people who say, 'We have this wonderful idea that will help seniors, all you have to do is give your blessings and $250,000.' We weren't asking for any money. We went in looking for understanding and support."

Jennings got it. After all, he was from a reputable company and was genuinely committed to making the lives of seniors a bit easier. More important, he got the names, addresses and phone numbers of every area director on aging.

In April, Southwestern Bell invited 110 of them to a meeting to explain what it had in mind, and also to offer an inducement to get them to go along with the idea. "We were going to put the first 30 to 40 pages of the directory at their disposal. We would let them put in whatever information they thought was necessary."

That decision ensured cooperation. No matter how

much funding an agency receives, it is never enough. And here was Southwestern Bell offering to take care of the problem that had plagued the St. Louis office on aging and its counterparts nationwide. The agencies had reams of information. They could tell seniors how to get free transportation to their doctor, the location of senior citizen centers where they could meet with people who shared their interests, and where they would be able to find housing, college courses and even jobs. But they had no easy way of getting that information out. Southwestern Bell had just offered a solution, and one that would not cost them anything.

"We truly believe that the information is vital," Jennings says. "And while we could have done it from public documents, we wanted to make sure the agencies were on our side." The move made selling the directory much easier, both in Southwestern Bell's core area and beyond. "When we moved beyond our five-state territory, we didn't want to be perceived as carpetbaggers."

The decision to turn over the front of the Silver Pages to the local area agency on aging cost virtually nothing. The agencies themselves would write the text; all Southwestern Bell had to do was typeset it and make sure that it was included in each book. But this simple move took care of any lingering public relations problems Southwestern Bell might have with the new directories, and it is no accident that the seal of the National Association of Area Agencies on Aging and their slogan, "Reaching the nation's elderly," is on the cover.

With the agencies' support behind him, Jennings started courting the seniors themselves. While they needed, and probably wanted, the information the agencies would provide, that was not going to be enough. Nobody rushes out to receive public service information.

The secret, Jennings quickly realized, would be putting together a directory that listed merchants who were willing to give discounts and/or special services to people over 60. "We had to give people a reason to take another directory into their homes," Jennings says. If he could, Southwestern Bell would have what company officials took to describing as a win-win-win situation. The seniors would win, because they would have a list of places where they would be charged less. The merchants could win by attracting more business.[1] And finally, Southwestern Bell would win by finding a new source of revenue.

The concept seemed fine. Retailers agreed to provide breaks to seniors and said they would advertise, providing Southwestern Bell could guarantee a large enough audience. That should be easy enough, Jennings figured. Surely all the NAAAA chapters, who were now willing to work with Southwestern Bell, kept lists, right?

Wrong. "Nobody had the names, except in Ohio," Jennings discovered. So Southwestern Bell spent months compiling its own lists, culled from state motor vehicle department records, solicitations with its monthly phone bills and setting up displays for the book in places seniors gather.

But having the names was not enough. Jennings

---

1. And, if they were smart, they could do it on particularly slow days. For example, hardware stores are mobbed on Saturdays, but virtually empty during the week. They could offer the 10 percent senior citizen discount on Tuesday, Wednesday and Thursday to balance out store traffic.

wanted to make sure those people would be expecting their copy of the Silver Pages. So, Southwestern Bell did something foreign to utility companies: It launched a massive advertising and publicity campaign.

In August 1984, the company held a press conference to formally announce plans for the Silver Pages and to explain its contents.

The first 40 pages or so would have the information provided by the local agencies on aging. Like the rest of the book, it would be printed in large type for easier reading.

The public service section would be followed by a general-interest magazine for seniors comprised of articles such as "Seniors and Computers" and "Educating Yourself about Insurance."

Then would come the heart of the book, at least from Southwestern Bell's perspective: hundreds of pages listing businesses and services that provided a discount for seniors. Everyone who did—from the accountant who offered a free income tax organizer to the yarn store that provided a 10 percent discount on all purchases—would receive a free listing that provided the name of their company, its address and phone number, plus up to five words describing the break it would give to people over 60.

Of course, those who wanted to have additional space were encouraged to do so. By the end of 1987 a full-page ad in the Silver Pages cost about $10,000.

In addition to describing the directories, the press conference was intended to show that Southwestern Bell had the support of the various agencies on aging. Both Lennie-Marie Tolliver, U.S. commissioner on aging, and Ray

Matalish, executive director of the NAAAA, spoke, praising both the directory and Southwestern Bell for creating it. Their comments were to become an integral part of the company's publicity efforts and were included in press releases the company sent to reporters. Indeed, virtually every time someone commented favorably about the book, Southwestern Bell—in sharp contrast to the normally self-effacing attitudes of utilities—was quick to spread the word.[2]

It was also at that press conference that Jennings announced plans to have the Silver Pages in 110 cities within two years—the first time a Baby Bell would try to take a product it had developed nationwide.

"There were two reasons for our rapid rollout," Jennings explained later. "We felt we had obligations to the 110 people we had brought in, to give them a directory as soon as possible." The second reason was less altruistic. Jennings was afraid of competition. And as it turned out, he had a right to be worried.

There is nothing proprietary about the Silver Pages. As Jennings pointed out, all the information provided by the area directors on aging is in the public domain. There would be nothing to stop another company—either a RBOC or another publisher—from coming up with a similar idea. While Southwestern Bell could, and did, protect the name "Silver Pages," anyone else could copy the concept, deciding to call their book the "Golden Pages" for example.

And if competitors didn't come to that realization

2. An example: The "Private Sector Initiative Award" the company had received from the U.S. Department of Health and Human Services for creating the Silver Pages would be blown up and included in subsequent directories.

themselves, there was a good chance that someone would tell them.

One of the dangers of talking to as many people as Southwestern Bell did in preparing the Silver Pages is that leaks are inevitable—and they are not always intentional. "At one of our first senior citizen meetings, after we explained the concept, someone said what a wonderful idea. We should tell Pacific Bell to do it," Jennings recalled. While Jennings tried to stress to the enthusiastic supporter that different parts of the old Bell system now compete with one another, he made sure that California was part of the initial rollout.

The rollout itself was relatively simple. Within its core five-state territory, the company drew on its existing salesforce to sell Silver Pages ads. Outside the area, it added salesmen whose sole job was to pitch advertising for the directory. Their jobs were made substantially easier by the millions Southwestern Bell spent on advertising; money that sometimes paid off in unexpected ways.

For example, prior to divestiture the Bell system had sponsored golfer Raymond Floyd on the pro tour. In exchange, he'd occasionally play a round of golf with major advertisers, do clinics and wear a visor with the Bell system logo on it during tournaments. That way every time he appeared on camera, AT&T got a subliminal plug.

After the breakup of AT&T, Southwestern Bell decided to sponsor Floyd, and promptly gave him a Silver Pages cap, a hat that was prominently displayed on the newspaper and magazine sports pages around the world in June 1986, when Floyd won the Masters.

It was hard to miss the tie-in. Every article mentioned that Floyd, then 42, was the oldest man ever to win the Masters, and there he was being sponsored by a product geared to older people.

"This is Bob 'Silver Tongue' Hope"

The advertising also took more conventional forms. Almost immediately after deciding to publish a senior citizens directory, Southwestern Bell concluded that it needed a big-name spokesman. The product, while unique, could be difficult to explain in a 30- or 60-second television spot. Using a star as spokesman would make it easier to draw attention to the complicated message. No surprise there. The reason companies sign up everyone from Bill Cosby to teenage heartthrob, Michael J. Fox, is to break through the clutter of television advertising.

But Southwestern Bell's requirements were a little bit more selective. The spokesman had to be over 60. After all, that was the target market. And since the product itself is not inherently interesting—it would have been far easier to advertise vacations or cars—it would help enormously if the spokesman was not only comfortable on camera, but could make the presentation interesting. In the best of all worlds, he would be able to make what could be a very dry subject amusing.

Who is the nation's most-loved senior citizen? A *People* magazine poll said Bob Hope. Would the then 80-year-old entertainer pitch the books? For a fee of well into the six figures annually he would be more than happy to stand up in front of the cameras and say things like:

This is Bob 'Silver Tongue' Hope here to tell you about the new Silver Pages, the senior citizens discount directory from Southwestern Bell Publications.

It's a complete specialty directory just for seniors who are looking for businesses that make special offers to those 60 and over. Everything seniors need to make their lives a little easier. Helpful information on agencies on aging, services, programs, transportation.

Where were those deals when I was 'on the road' with you know who?

And that's just up front, before you even get to the real 'stars' of the book: businesses with colorful messages for seniors.

I asked George Burns about his mature outlook and he said he was out looking for girls. Others offer discounts on everything from arts and crafts to restaurants to travel. [He thumbs through the book.] Here's one right down my fairway—golf courses.

The Silver Pages, where businesses say welcome to senior citizens.

I wonder if they have any good jokes at a discount? Hi-ho Silver.

All the preparation, and the advertising, paid off when the books debuted in the second half of 1985. "The initial response from seniors was overwhelming," Jennings recalled. "From the advertisers we got a reasonable acceptance, but a lot of wait-and-see attitude." They waited, saw and became convinced. In its second year, pages and revenues were up 40 percent and the company expects to start making a profit on the directories in early 1988, which is right on schedule.

"We think the potential return, in five to ten years, is in the range of the Yellow Pages."

That means Jennings expects that the Silver Pages will be generating more than $500 million in revenues—and more than $100 million in profits—in the foreseeable future.

But wait a second. This is a utility we are talking about.

Would the Silver Pages have been a success prior to divestiture? Jennings answers the question almost before it is asked: "No, I don't think there is any chance. First of all, we would not have done it on a national basis, and if the Bell system decided to do it, the Silver Pages would have ended up looking twenty-three different ways, all the regional companies and AT&T would have done it differently, because that is just the way that we were. Fifteen of the local phone companies would have ended up saying, 'Hell, I don't have to do a separate book. I'll put in a section for seniors in my directory,' if they bought in that far."

So how come Southwestern Bell, staffed with people who are products of the kind of thinking that Jennings just ridiculed, was able to pull it off? After all, you don't think of people who work for the phone company when you are trying to compile a list of entrepreneurs.

Jennings smiles. "You are stereotyping us all. Most of us who grew up in directory don't know any more about the phone company than you do. I don't know anything about the phone company. Typically in our history, guys in the phone company who were ticketed for big jobs would get a little smattering of directory experience, because some day it might be part of their responsibility. But it was very rare for one of us to go to the phone company."

Jennings lowers his voice, and leans forward as if he is about to whisper a secret. "And the reason it was rare for us to go to the phone company was, we didn't want to go. Directory has always been a fun business. Yeah, it was part of the telephone company, but it was selling, traveling, and it was a hell of a good time and we were successful. Most of the people here grew up in directory and we never, except on paper, thought about ourselves as being part of the phone company. Our paycheck came from there, but we didn't think about the same things."

Once the shackles of being a utility were removed, they had a chance to prove it. The company gambled relatively large sums of money—depending on its size, it costs between $500,000 and $1.5 million to publish a Silver Pages for one city—and appears to have won.

The strong start also seems to have preempted any competition; Jennings expects to have the field to himself for years to come. "I don't think anyone will make the commitment in terms of resources that we have made, now that we are there." He just doesn't think the market is big enough to support two national senior directories.

The initial evidence proves him right. "What has happened is that almost every directory now includes a special senior pages section, which, frankly, helps us as far as I am concerned. If they have 50 people on the street telling businesses why they ought to advertise to seniors, that in my mind makes it an easier sale for us.

"If the advertiser is convinced by us, or our competitors, that he should advertise to seniors, then it comes down to who has the best delivery mechanism."

And if that is the question, then Southwestern Bell is going to win hands down. It offers a full directory for seniors when everyone else is just offering a special section. With the Silver Pages, advertisers get a place in a medium that is dedicated to seniors, as opposed to placing their ads in an all-purpose telephone directory. Obviously, that is much more appealing.

To underscore the directory's appeal, Jennings continues to add inducements for people to use the book. Through a tie-in with VISA, people who receive the Silver Pages can also get a special credit card that offers them up to $300,000 in insurance every time they fly and they can also receive substantial discounts on travel. Other programs are also planned.

There is a tendency for new businesses, or ones like Southwestern Bell who have never done it before, to think of marketing as a black art. As Jennings and his staff showed, marketing, at its core, isn't really that difficult to understand. You figure out who you want to sell to—in this case, senior citizens—and then you determine what inducements are needed to get them to buy.

If you approach marketing with this targeted attitude, even if you are selling something with the sex appeal of a phone book, you can make a lot of money.

6 | The art of copying: "How to be a fast second"

Leslie H. Wexner is in the middle of explaining how he created his 3,000-store retailing empire when the phone rings.

It is Verna Gibson, president of the 257 Limited stores that are the heart of Wexner's $3-billion company, and Gibson is upset. She has just seen the results of a consumer survey in which an overwhelming number of Limited's shoppers complained that prices were too high.

Wexner talks to her for a minute, and Gibson hangs up happy. "I told Verna to think about what they were saying and see if it made any sense," explains Wexner, as always impeccably turned out in clothes cut a bit slimmer and in colors just a shade brighter than those an investment banker would wear. "Her sales, earnings and prices points are all the highest they have ever been. That means women can't think the prices are too high. If they did, they wouldn't shop there. The results of the survey would have been the same if Mercedes Benz sent me a questionnaire asking what I thought about their cars. I'd tell them their prices were too high. And what car would I buy next time? A Mercedes Benz."

That, in a nutshell, explains Wexner's attitude toward traditional marketing techniques. He's against them.

He doesn't believe in market surveys like the one Gib-

LESLIE H. WEXNER of The Limited

son took. He won't advertise, because "nobody has ever proven to me that it pays," and he doesn't believe in focus groups.

To Wexner, all those traditional marketing techniques are crutches to be used by those who don't have a "feel" for their business. That makes him different from other marketing stars. Obviously they, too, have an implicit understanding of what should work, an understanding that stems from their intelligence and experience. But they rely on the research tools Wexner scoffs at to confirm what they think consumers will want.

For Wexner, no confirmation is necessary. To him, great retailers are like great artists. They instinctively know what to do. Pablo Picasso (Wexner owns some of his sketchbooks) didn't need market research to do great work and neither does Leslie Wexner.

But Wexner's art is different, more subtle, and for those of us not blessed with the ability of a Picasso, a lot easier to emulate.

When we think about "stars" in the field of art, business, or anything else, there is a tendency to picture people whose ability appears to be God-given—people like Akio Morita, chairman of Sony, who take a blank piece of paper and create something that has never been before.

Morita was walking down a Tokyo street when he suddenly wondered why he couldn't stroll and listen to his beloved classical music at the same time. Why can't we take one of our high-quality transistor radios, build in a tape recorder and add powerful earphones, he asks himself. If we did, we'd have a portable, personal stereo. Thus, the Walkman was born.

And it is more than possible that the first song you heard coming out of your Walkman was Carole King's "You've Got a Friend," which served as the anthem of a generation a few years back. "It really is a great song," says King. "I can say that, because I don't feel as if I wrote it. It is just something that flowed through me onto the page."

This, too, is a wonderful story, but like Morita's tale of the Walkman, it is hard to learn anything from it. In each case the creative process can't be easily translated to others. You can teach Morita's knowledge of electronics, or King's understanding of music to someone, but they won't create a Walkman or songs. It is, as Yogi Berra said in another context, "impossible to hit and think at the same time."

But Wexner doesn't have the ability of a Picasso, a King, or a Berra for that matter. His skill isn't innate. He isn't a fashion designer. What he is, in his words, is "a very fast second." He takes things others *have already created* and makes little changes in them in ways that he believes will appeal to women.

It isn't creation. It is copying. But so sure is Wexner that he knows what to copy, that he doesn't need to conduct market research.

And if there were ever a place to do market research, the creation of Victoria's Secret was it.

Victoria's Secret is intended to be "every woman's fantasy of what a lingerie store should be. Someplace small, intimate, a store that is probably English, or French or Viennese," Wexner says. How did he know that was the fantasy? He didn't. He just made it up. How did he know the stores should be done in pink tile, gray carpeting and soft lighting, or that it should have classical music playing at all times? He made that up too. And how did a then 47-year-old bachelor from Columbus, Ohio, whose mother has an office across the hall from him in The Limited's executive suite, decide on what to stock in these fantasy stores? Did he survey women? Study other stores? Look at projections of lingerie sales?

Nope. Wexner—whose empire now accounts for 7 percent of all the clothing bought by American women—did what he always does when contemplating a new venture. He sat at the conference table in his office and looked at the hundreds of photographs he had taken over the years. The photographs could be of a sign fixture in Europe, the display window of a bookstore in Italy, or the menu board at a McDonald's in Japan. In the case of Victoria's Secret, rarely did they have anything to do with lingerie, or women's clothing for that matter. He played with the photographs for a couple of years as he went about tending to the day-to-day affairs at The Limited, Inc., and then, seemingly out of nowhere, poof! The prototype for Victoria's Secret sprang into being.

All of this takes a bit of explaining, but the first thing you have to keep in mind is that Leslie Howard Wexner, a man who now has three or four stores in virtually every shopping mall in America, never planned to be a retailing potentate.

His parents ran a full-line women's department store in Columbus, and Wexner, who grew up stocking shelves and washing windows, realized two things after graduating from Ohio State. First, the store was never going to be able comfortably to support both him and his parents, and second, he might not need to stock everything his parents did.

About the time he graduated, the "preppie look," as personified by the J.G. Hook line of clothes, was becoming popular, so in 1963 Wexner borrowed $5,000 from an aunt to open a shop *limited* to women's sportswear. Its success allowed him to open another, which in turn gave him the cash to open a third, and so it went. By the time he was 30, Wexner had 6 stores. His ambition was to have 50, or maybe 100, before he died. "I daydreamed of having $20 million in revenues. When I talked about it, people thought I was absolutely mad.

"There wasn't a master plan. I don't think most entrepreneurs have one. I don't think that Ray Kroc [who built the McDonald's empire] ever said 'I think we will have 6,000 stores around the world,' I think it is right foot, left foot."

So Wexner started putting one foot in front of the other and soon—helped in large part by a public offering —he found he was running out of room to walk. His idea of specializing in stylish, relatively inexpensive sportswear had caught on even better than it had in his daydreams. Soon he had more than 100 Limited stores and "we realized that by the early or mid-1980s there would be a Limited virtually every place there could be one."

It was only then that Wexner decided to diversify. But, surprised by his success, and doubting that he could do it again, Wexner set out to find the absolute safest business to add. "The easiest business to be in is the business you are already in," he says. "So we decided we should have another specialty-store business and one that used the same recipe, if you will. Oatmeal chocolate chip with raisins, as opposed to chocolate chips with raisins. We began to conceptualize The Limited Express which, even in its name, is as close as you can get to The Limited without being exactly the same."

Where The Limited caters to young women, The Limited Express focused on an even younger market, primarily teenagers, and it quickly recorded hundreds of millions of sales on its own. "Then Lane Bryant [a then struggling chain that sells fashionable clothing to larger women] came up for sale. We read about it in the *Wall Street Journal*. The question was, could you transfer specialty-store skills from the young-minded, regularly sized customer to a special-size customer and, yeah, I thought we could. Now, that may seem obvious, but I was scared that when we bought Lane Bryant, we couldn't transfer our skills, that their base of production, stores, customers and services were not transferable. It would be like GM saying we make a Chevrolet, I don't know if we can make this thing called a Pontiac, it's different."

It wasn't, of course, but that worry and self-doubt are a hallmark of everything Wexner does. Even though he relies on instinct—or maybe *because* he relies so heavily on instinct—he broods about every move he makes. Once he makes a decision, there is no doubt and Wexner will open as many stores as he can, as quickly as he can. But getting to that point takes a long time. No ready, fire, aim for him.

"I'll give you a contrast," he says. "If you look at the other specialty-store companies like U.S. Shoe [the large St. Louis-based holding company], you'll see they came out differently than we did. They said their skill was operating specialty stores so they then go from shoe stores to women's stores, to men's stores, to home-improvement stores, to drug stores. Anything that they can define as a specialty store. And you can see that the reasoning is impeccable. They are saying, 'We know how to run specialty stores. The optical business is a fashion business just like retailing, therefore eyeglass stores are just like shoe stores, and we can successfully operate an optical chain.' "

The reasoning may or may not be impeccable. It is reminiscent of the thinking that dominated business in the 1960s, when executives, in essence, said: If you can run one business, you can run them all. As a result, huge conglomerates—like ITT, which owned everything from hotels to insurance companies to bakeries—were assembled with decidedly mixed results.

But right or wrong it is not thinking Wexner is comfortable with.[1] "I don't have that facility. I think these are real different businesses. Someone said to me a while ago, why don't we sell cookies? We know how to sell, we know how to market, let's open cookie stores. I said I don't understand how to do that."

Have camera, will travel

All the while he is thinking about cookies, or trying to figure out how to clone The Limited, or pondering whether selling clothes to large women makes sense,

1. Indeed, for the longest time the only business he was comfortable with was specialty retailing for women. It was only in 1987 that Wexner announced that he would experiment with opening specialty retail shops for men.

Wexner is looking at the 35mm pictures he has taken on his travels around the world. He reaches into the pile on the conference table and picks out one at random. It's of a Japanese store that sells nothing but cotton and silk items. He becomes a bit defensive when asked to explain the picture's significance. "Over the last 10 years, I probably have spent 60 or 80 days walking around mindlessly looking at stores throughout the world, photographing things I like. Then I sit here and look at this crap," he says, gesturing to the photos on the table. "I can't even tell you why I took most of these pictures. They interested me at the time, but I can't remember why."

But he can explain why he takes the photos in the first place.

With the various retailing concepts he creates, "I am trying to invent something that does not exist and I read somewhere that there are three kinds of creativity. Imitation—copying something and doing it as well as the original. I see that as very creative. Second, innovation: Taking something and adding an element and making it better. And finally, pure imagination. Leonardo da Vinci had that."

By this definition, it is clear that Wexner doesn't see himself as imaginative. But that does not bother him in the least.

"My skill is the ability to put ideas together. If you give me a blank piece of paper, I will give you a blank piece of paper back. I find imitating and innovating a creative exercise. What I am able to do is take a couple of different ideas and merge them so they appear to be something different. And I think that is what artists do."

Innovation is certainly easier to accomplish than pure

invention. It is simpler to look at a big, bulky sweater and say that it should come in bright colors, than it is to try to determine what kind of sweater women want this week. But, although it is simpler, it requires the constant juxtaposing of ideas. To find them, Wexner travels. Constantly. "I logged 600 hours *in the air* last year alone," he says. And when he lands he "schleps around with a camera, taking hundreds of pictures and putting ideas together."

You can see the results in Victoria's Secret. The idea that would lead to the lingerie chain first surfaced in the early 1980s, when Wexner visited a small lingerie store in England called Courtney's. "It was very British," he recalls. "Everything was in boxes that the saleswoman would hand to you, but there was something about the feeling of the store, the intimacy, I liked."

None of The Limited-owned chains had sold lingerie up to this point, and they wouldn't as a result of Wexner's visit to Courtney's. He took some pictures—it would have been surprising if he hadn't—and returned home.

About two years later, one of Wexner's executives went on a business trip to the West Coast, during which he stopped in San Francisco and visited a tiny, five-store chain called Victoria's Secret. When he came back, he told Wexner about what he had seen. It sounded interesting, so on his next trip West, Wexner, who spends six or eight days a year just wandering through retail stores run by others, decided to take a look. What he saw intrigued him.

Judging by the silence coming from the cash register, it was clear the stores weren't making money. And Wexner didn't care for their look, which featured red brick and frosted glass. Still, Wexner walked away happy. While wandering about the stores he had been struck with what sounds like a very mundane marketing insight: "Most women wear underwear most of the time." Selling lingerie, he thought, might be an opportunity.

"The lingerie business, by the nature of the product and the customer, is very similar to the apparel business, but I had never thought about it," Wexner says. "When you ask what businesses are similar to what we are doing, you might say shoes, or jewelry. People think of other products of outerwear, or other ages or sizes we could go after, but for whatever reason people—including me—never thought about innerwear."

Even though he now realized that lingerie could provide a market for The Limited, Wexner still wasn't ready to move. After visiting the stores, he called the founder and owner of Victoria's Secret, Roy Raymond, to say he admired his concept and suggested that they meet. Not surprisingly, Raymond was skeptical. He was afraid Wexner would steal his idea. But "I invited him to Columbus to see our systems and organizations and see if there was anything that we could help him with. I didn't think we had any nuclear secrets."

Two or three months later, in late 1982, Raymond came to visit and the more he talked, the more intrigued Wexner became. "When I met Roy, and he told me a little bit about how the lingerie business worked and who his customers were, I was fascinated. His business was never profitable so, from a business point of view, the idea wasn't working. But, from the customer point of view, it was. They were coming in the store and buying. Even though his sales weren't terrific, they were significant and he did have five stores and a catalog business. He had all that with an operation that was being run by an amateur. He bought in ones and twos. Things he bought might stay on the shelves for two years and he had no idea what were the popular items.

"Still, I could just see enormous potential. I think what Roy discovered by accident—and I don't think he realized what he had discovered—is that nobody had looked at lingerie as a specialty-store concept. It had always been treated by generalists, operated as a department within a department store."

Wexner is quite right. Lingerie had always been thought of as an item of utility, not fashion. "Here was a wonderful opportunity to differentiate and add value to a product that had been overlooked.

"My first thought was: Oh, my God, everywhere there is a Limited store there can be a Victoria's Secret. The reason for that is simple. If most women wear lingerie most of the time, then most of our customers are always buying lingerie and innerwear. That means our customer and the Victoria's Secret customer are the same."

Another executive might have made Raymond an offer on the spot, or instantly made plans to start a lingerie chain of his own. But Wexner doesn't work like that. He spent a while thinking about the conversation with Raymond. Then he went back to running The Limited—a six-day-a-week occupation for him, and therefore for his senior staff—and visiting retail stores run by others. He wanted to think about lingerie stores a bit longer. As we have seen, this is not a man who moves quickly. On his travels, he stumbled on a second insight that turned out to be as important as the realization that most women wear underwear most of the time.

"I looked in department stores and saw how they sold lingerie. It hangs there like salami. Here you have the sexiest product in the world for women, the most intimate product there is, and the way they are selling it is appalling. I said to myself, 'This could be a big opportunity. I wonder if you could make a living just selling lingerie.' "

Now, nearly three years after Wexner had visited Courtney's in England, things were beginning to fall into place. He was finally convinced that The Limited should sell lingerie. Since Raymond already had a lingerie business going, Wexner figured the fastest way to get underway would be to buy Victoria's Secret. But Raymond wasn't selling. He was planning to bring in venture capital and was thinking about going public. So Wexner began mentally designing the perfect lingerie store. Something small, intimate, decidedly feminine. Then, six months later when Wexner had a pretty good idea of what he wanted, "out of the clear blue, Raymond called back and said he had changed his mind and he wanted to sell. Would we come to San Francisco, right away?"

It was then that Wexner, who had spent more than 1,000 days thinking about the idea of having a specialty lingerie store, made his move. He went to San Francisco and, within a day, he and Raymond had a deal. The Limited had entered the lingerie business.

What he did not do

Before explaining how Wexner built Victoria's Secret into what has become the fastest-growing concept in retail history, it is interesting to note what he did not do.

He did not copy Raymond's idea: he bought it. At first blush, the decision to buy, not build, appears out of character. Wexner created his empire by copying and then improving on the ideas of others. His first store in suburban Columbus was nothing more than a copy of what J.G. Hook was doing, and throughout the years, in all of his stores, Wexner has made a habit of spotting a fashion trend early and then producing lower-priced copies of it.

Why not do that with Victoria's Secret? There was nothing proprietary about the idea of setting up stores to sell lingerie. He could have hedged his bets even further by setting up Victoria's Secret-like departments in his existing stores. If they proved successful—and remember that no matter how intriguing Raymond's concept, he had never made money with it—Wexner could then expand the departments.

"That has been done," Wexner says in dismissing the conservative approach he could have taken. "You put a little stand in and sell Maidenform bras two styles, two colors, all sizes. Merchandising lingerie as a specialty store, as opposed to a department, makes it better because it really is a special item. Just the words we use, 'intimate apparel,' show that this is a very personal, special item.

"Besides, Victoria's Secret already consisted of five stores. It wasn't a theoretical thing. It was a business that had already been invented and the consumer had accepted. Why would you want to fix something that wasn't broken?"

Well, it may not have been broken, but it certainly wasn't working very well. There were few financial controls and the company wasn't really sure what was selling. But to Wexner those problems were part of Victoria's Secret's appeal. After building three or four specialty companies, Wexner knew how to improve things quickly. And there was a lot to improve.

"Their merchandising concept was they went to lingerie manufacturers and bought pretty things. Wonderful bras, panties, whatever. But it wasn't professionally bought. It was stocked as if a woman who had virtually no limit on her credit cards was buying for herself. That looks nice, let's buy one of these and one of those.

"If you went from store to store, you didn't see much continuity. If somebody wanted to buy two of virtually anything, they couldn't, because it wouldn't be in stock.

"And no one ever asked, 'Of every dollar women spend on lingerie, how much is spent on bras and how many and what kinds of bras do they buy? What colors? What are the most popular sizes? Are $300 negligees good things to sell?' So we started asking those things, and finding out what makes a lingerie business."

So what makes a lingerie business?

The answers, at least in the most general terms, are surprisingly simple. "Size 32–34 bras in B and C cups are maybe 80 percent of the bra business," says Wexner. "And no matter what anybody says, most people buy white." Those simple findings—ones that Wexner says Roy Raymond never paid enough attention to—gave him a starting point, at least. But knowing what size the items should be is one thing, what specific garments they should be is quite another. And that is a critical question. In retailing, buying is really selling. If you buy merchandise your customers like, you'll make money. If you don't, those clothes will sit on the shelf forever. In determining what to stock, Wexner did what he always does in deciding what merchandise to sell. He invented a customer.

What would Cybill Shepherd think?

"When we started The Limited in 1963 with preppie clothes, I had in mind some fictional collegiate who went to Connecticut College for Women." Some years later, Hollywood finally gave Wexner the exact image he wanted. "She was Ali MacGraw in *Love Story*. And the question I always asked in buying merchandise was, Would she buy it? I was always banging my head against the question, would [the Ali MacGrawesque character] buy this sweater or blouse.

"With Victoria's Secret, the customer is Cybill Shepherd, because I think most women 20 to 40, if they could be anybody today, would be Cybill Shepherd. Not Barbie Benton.

"Maybe it's bullshit. Ten years ago I would have said Charlie, the advertising fiction [a tall, slim, independent career woman in her twenties who is not above patting her beau on the backside in public]. Today, everybody wants to be Shepherd, because she is naughty, but nice. Free-spirited. Has a good figure but she's not a *Playboy* bunny. She's more than 30 years old. She is very much her own person, but she is still pretty and sexy.

" 'Would Cybill Shepherd buy this?' is the question I

always tell the buyers to keep in mind. In two years, five years, seven years, maybe it isn't Cybill Shepherd, it's whomever. But today it is."

Wexner understands that his basic premise—the idea that Cybill Shepherd is about to walk into her local mall and buy lingerie at a Victoria's Secret—is flawed. "For all I know, she doesn't wear any underwear," he concedes. "But to personalize your customer is a good idea. Having that image of your customer avoids the problem of carrying everything from Frederick's of Hollywood's crotchless lingerie to flannel gowns. All you have to do is ask, 'Would Cybill buy it?'"

But in what kind of store would Cybill be making those purchases? Wexner describes the five stores he acquired as having a "bawdy, bedroom look to them. Lots of red velvet and dark oak furniture. They had etched glass and etched mirrors. It didn't have a quality image or an intimate look. In harsh terms, it almost had a red-light-district appearance." Clearly, this was not the kind of place where Cybill Shepherd would shop.

Wexner wanted to give the stores a more classic, classy feel. "The notion was kind of vague, but I thought every woman's fantasy would be to shop in a European lingerie store. Maybe it is a French lingerie store, maybe it is an English lingerie store, maybe Viennese. There is a certain tradition of good taste and quality that goes with that."

And his first thoughts about how to create that fantasy store were what they always are. He wanted to copy an existing concept. "We figured we'd go to Europe, find the store, photograph it and Xerox it," Wexner said about his initial plan. The problem was that after months of touring Europe, he couldn't find a store to copy. "We went to England, France, Vienna, trying to find that fantasy store. We saw a lot of lingerie shops, but typically they would have no displays. Europeans went for concealed stock in pretty paisley boxes on the shelves. Everything was sold to the customer. Nobody could touch it. That is sort of old-fashioned European retailing. But the stores did have an intimacy because they were small and pretty and matched the product."

So Wexner set out to create an intimate store. What should it look like? His premise was simple, if not humble. "We asked, 'If we could get all of our customers together and get inside their heads and say let's create a fantasy lingerie store, what would it look like?'

"Well, it wouldn't have a high tech atmosphere. It would be European and feminine with lots of pinks and peaches. Soft lighting. A bathrobe in the fitting room. Carpeting throughout. Pink marble, not Formica. The acid test of if we succeeded would be: If all the product was taken out, people would still say, 'This must be a lingerie store.' Nobody would guess that it sold sweaters, or men's clothing."

And that is exactly what Wexner created. All Victoria's Secret stores—which range in size from a snug 2,000 square feet up to a still-far-from-huge 4,000 square feet—have exactly the appointments he envisaged. Classical music plays at all times, and the stores smell of the sachets that are scattered about.

But why, if you are trying to create every woman's fantasy of what a lingerie store should be, don't you ask women? Why create a mythical shopper like Cybill Shepherd—who may be as far from the average Victoria's

Secret customer as you can get—when you can gather a representative sample of your potential market and ask them what they want?

"You can't create a new idea that way," Wexner says. "Focus groups can be used to bang ideas off and get some sensitivity to an idea. But a focus group would create an Edsel.

"Let's assume a world where there are no fast-food restaurants, and you asked people, 'Where would you like to buy a hamburger?' They'd describe a better Howard Johnson's, or a restaurant that would serve a better hamburger. They'd never invent McDonald's.

"I don't think focus groups can conceptualize new products because new products are outside of everyone's frame of reference. So what they give you is incremental improvements on what exists. Or you get an Edsel, something that is simply dumb."

And yet the vast majority of Wexner's competitors use focus groups, customer surveys and extensive market research before they make a decision. Are they just wasting time and money?

"In businesses where people don't have the touch or feel—the art, if you will—the only way they can get a new product is with market research and surveys. That is the safest course for them. If something goes wrong, they can always point to the numbers to justify their decision."

But that is not how chief executives should make decisions, Wexner quickly adds. "The role of the innovator, the creative guy, is to conceptualize something. The guy who created Federal Express didn't create mail, or airplanes. He just put them together in a creative way. You could never have invented that by talking to customers. You could have listened to complaints: 'I can't get a package delivered the next day,' and that sort of thing. Customers would have been able to describe around the problem, but they never would have told you to create a system that guarantees next-day delivery."

But notice the kind of creativity Wexner is describing. He is not talking about inventing something that has never been. "Maybe one in a million can do that," he says. "In my industry, it would be people like Coco Chanel or Giorgio Armani. I know I can't do that. But I do know I can put things together. If I see enough things, I can put them together so that one and one make three. I can merge ideas, innovate. And I am not reluctant to imitate at all. Ego does not get in my way. I will absolutely Xerox something. In the industry, we call it knocking it off, and it sounds stupid, but there are very few people who know what to knock off.

"Our business is to track fashion, to know where it is going, as opposed to pushing it out or inventing it. I see that instinct to invent every once in a while in some of our buyers. They wouldn't articulate this, but they really want to be designers. One out of a million, or one of ten million, have that ability.

"I would describe myself as creative, but the creativity does not go into the invention of the product. The creativity goes to the marketing of the product; its packaging. The invention of the three-arm sweater wouldn't do much for me. But, if someone invented it, I would be very intrigued about how do we sell more three-arm sweaters than anyone in the world.

"The way I explain it to myself is that I am interested

in the business of fashion. I am not interested in fashion. I have never been to a Paris fashion show. I don't have the curiosity to see one. Verna Gibson says I see everything in burgundy and navy. That's a little bit of an exaggeration, but not much. I have been at meetings where people say next spring the hot color will be flamingo pink and I never got very excited about that. I am not fascinated with the invention at the product level. I am fascinated with the marketing of the products that have been invented."

That is a good assessment of Wexner's style. His fascination—what he considers marketing—consists of recognizing far earlier than most of his competitors can what people will want, and then figuring out how to give it to them in the most inexpensive way. The presentation is elegant. On a recent tour of a Victoria's Secret store, Wexner—who arrived half an hour late, as usual—complained that the boxes some of the lingerie came in were not pretty enough. But the price tag never comes close to the items he has knocked off. The secret is to be out quickly, and come as close to the original as you can. When Wexner saw the preppie look becoming fashionable again recently, he invented the Hunter's Run brand which is featured at The Limited stores. When people wanted European-style active sportswear, Wexner introduced the Forenza line. When Australia became "in," in the mid-1980s, suddenly The Limited, Inc. was there with Outback Red, sold by mannequins in safari outfits.

"It may be self-effacing, but I think I see myself and my skills accurately, and I don't have a lot of skills," Wexner says. "I am very content being a fast second, once the idea has been invented."

"This is where the art comes in "

When he finds an idea that intrigues him, like the selling of woman's lingerie, he mulls it over, thinks about what exists and what he can add to it. And then, after what can seem like endless deliberation, after he has finally figured out what has to be done, he moves quickly. In the case of Victoria's Secret, that meant opening 250 stores in just three years. But the decision about what has to be done doesn't come from analyzing reports from "experts" predicting where the market is going. "I think it has to come from trusted instinct about the future of where *you* think the market is going. That is where the art comes in and I do think retailing is an art."

That belief explains Wexner's aversion to market research—the numbers only quantify what has happened in the past. They don't give a good feel for the future. It also explains his refusal to run more than an occasional ad while his competitors spend millions on advertising.

"We do some," Wexner says almost sheepishly. "We periodically advertise a brand or an item in magazines. Express has done it, and we have done it with Forenza. But we philosophically believe in spending the money on the store and on the things the customers see in the stores.

"We have tested general media advertising, and we have never figured out how it really works," he adds. "We can't prove that on a regular basis we can do it well enough to get a payback. Maybe that's because we have never done a good ad. We are always testing, but we haven't seen results to justify it."

The fact that this is contrary to the strategy of other

retailers—especially department stores—doesn't bother Wexner. In fact, he seems to relish the difference.

"I am not sure that advertising works for them either," he says. "They are not models of sterling success. Besides, their economics are different than ours. When Macy's runs a two-page ad, it is not only advertising the specific item, it is also advertising to bring traffic into the whole store. The thought is if your wife is stimulated by the ad to come in and look at sheets, maybe she'll also buy a dress. Our market is so targeted, and our store volume is so much smaller, that we are either right with an ad, or we get a zero.

"But I think I am 'righter' the first time. I am not so sure that advertising works for them. An example: Every two weeks they advertise they have beds on sale, and once every fifteen years, when you need a bed, you pay attention. That is not very efficient, is it? I think if department stores knew how to spend their dollars wisely on the store, on their displays, they would do better. But if they can't do that in a way that will stimulate sales, the simplest thing to do is get down and dirty and use price promotion.

"I think a huge part of retailing is the art. I am a merchant, and I am proud to be one, and the merchant part of the business is really the art. Knowing what to stock and how to display it, having the feel for the business. Verna Gibson can tell me what color will be hot a year or two from now, but she can't tell me why. She just has the instinct.

"Very few of the other major retailing companies are run by merchants. They are fifth generation, who are typically led by Harvard MBAs who have much better analytical and administrative skills than I do, but they are not merchants. And what comes out of that is a kind of disrespect, or a lack of confidence, in merchandising instinct. If you are not the artist, you have to depend on something. Numbers are wonderful, but they are not the way you make decisions about what to stock or what your stores should look like.

"I think the real secret of our success is not that I am a merchant, but that the presidents of our stores are merchants, and we will not compromise that.

"Think about another industry. Iacocca really likes cars. When GM has a problem, they don't go back to the product, their instinct is to go by EDS, or buy back the stock. They might have more efficient managers, but Iacocca will continue to trounce them."

Wexner sincerely believes everything he says about "the art" being a pivotal part of the retailing business, but it is important not to take those comments strictly at face value. While it is true that many of his ideas come from juxtaposing snapshots that have nothing in common, the business is not entirely haphazard. Consider again the matter of advertising.

Advertising is designed to do two things: To tell people about what you are selling, and to do so in such a way as to inspire them to buy. All retailers advertise. Even Wexner. While Macy's or Mervyn's may advertise through commercials on radio and TV and in newspapers and magazines, Wexner does his advertising a different way. He does it through the look and location of his stores.

Virtually every store The Limited owns—be it a Limited, Limited Express, Lerner Store or Victoria's Secret —is in a shopping mall. So, Wexner doesn't need to advertise to attract shoppers, the traffic is already there. And while it is true that Wexner would like to attract every woman who walks by, "I am not so much worried about the customers we don't have as the ones that we do.

"That really showed up when the business was small and I was trying to figure out how to do more business," he adds. "I was standing on the floor of Kingsdale, the first store, and it occurred to me the problem wasn't the number of people who walked in the store. The problem was the number who walked out empty-handed. If 10 percent of the people who walked out with nothing had bought, it would have made a drastic difference in our sales. I mulled that idea over for a long time."

The result was an inordinate amount of attention to the look and feel of the store, all designed to keep the customer in the store longer and encourage her to buy. Here Wexner leaves nothing to chance. At Victoria's Secret, as at the rest of the specialty shops he owns, store managers receive an elaborate floor plan every two weeks that describes in exact detail how their merchandise should be displayed for the next fourteen days. Every two weeks the customer should feel that everything in the store is new. Bored customers don't buy.

But, although the displays constantly change at Victoria's Secret, the purpose remains the same: Wexner is trying to create the perfect fantasy environment for buying lingerie.

And like many fantasies, Victoria's Secret involves sex. The covers of Victoria's Secret mail-order catalogs frequently feature the intertwined bodies of partially clad men and women. Many of the pictures on the inside feature couples in bed in positions that can only be described as post-coital and a good number of the displays leave little to the imagination. If the catalog were a movie, it would be rated with a very hard "R."

Not surprisingly, this is by design. "We are not Frederick's of Hollywood," Wexner says. "Their image is to purposely sell naughty underwear. Lingerie by its very nature is sexy. All the images: gossamer, billowy see-through negligees, black bikinis are very sexy, but that doesn't mean it is pornographic.

"The great artists painted a lot of nudes and Hugh Hefner photographs them and there is a judgmental line when you are talking about beauty in human form and pornography. It is a matter of degree. The question is when does a dream become a nightmare. I am not sure, but I know when I am having a nightmare.

"I worry that we may go from sexy and fantasy to explicit and pornographic," he adds. "But again, you are talking about the art department. I know sexy pictures sell more merchandise than dull pictures. Pictures of bras that show cleavage sell more bras to women than those that don't. But if they get too sexy, then they don't sell because everyone says that you are looking at erotica. You are talking about judgment."

And the judgment is Wexner's. He decides how the lingerie should be photographed—exactly how low on her waist can the male model place his hand, for example. That is combined with his businessman's judgment as to how the lingerie should be made.

When Wexner bought Victoria's Secret, almost everything in the store had a designer label. Soon, every label will say Victoria's Secret.

"What we are trying to do is develop a brand that has its own integrity and identity," Wexner says. It is a strategy he has used before. At The Limited, for example, he created the Forenza and Outback Red brands. "We are trying to develop a brand, because there is no brand name that covers everything we sell. Some people make lingerie, some make foundations, others make robes and nightwear. But there is no one single brand that pulls it all together with the same standard of quality and price."

Eliminating the middleman

The advantages of that are obviously twofold. First, if you make all the merchandise yourself, your margins will be better. There is no middleman to pay. The Limited owns Mast Industries, which manufactures a great deal of its merchandise.

The second advantage of making everything yourself is the creation of brand loyalty. "If you like Pontiacs, you can only buy them from a Pontiac dealer," is the way Wexner puts it. "If we take brand X, and make it very important, and everyone else has access to brand X, then we are only developing and cultivating that brand for the benefit of our competitors, since you can buy it everywhere." By creating the Victoria's Secret brand, Wexner establishes a captive audience. If you want a Victoria's Secret-brand product, you can only get it at a Victoria's Secret store.

Would he sell Victoria's Secret merchandise to others? Say, to a department store?

"We have no intention of doing that," Wexner replies.

"We probably could do it, but that is a whole other business. If you start selling a brand, you have gone from developing a brand to being a brand manager and being a wholesaler. I don't think that is our skill. And I am not sure department stores—or anyone who would consider themselves a competitor—would want to buy from us. I floated the idea by them once, and the notion of having to send checks to Columbus, Ohio, sent them wild."

So that leaves Wexner all alone in Columbus, looking at pictures and making money, through a combination of art and business sense. It is certainly true that he has a feel for his market and a wonderful intuitive sense of what his stores should look like. But it is also true that he understands the financial aspects of the business far better than he is willing to admit. He has learned that the shopping malls are the best place for his stores, and if you have more than 3,000 stores, you have gained some expertise in negotiating leases and have earned some clout with real estate developers.

And while it is true that Wexner understands what makes lingerie attractive to a woman, he also knows enough to make the most of it himself, thereby increasing the amount of money he makes on each sale.

These are all skills that have improved with practice and experience, and the results are seen in the success of Victoria's Secret. "The Limited was about fifteen years old before it reached the number of stores and dollar volume that we have with Victoria's Secret," he says. "So we have done in three years what took The Limited fifteen."

But isn't there an irony in all of this?

Here you have a middle-aged unmarried man living

in Columbus, Ohio, deciding the fantasies of women nationwide. Even Wexner concedes it is odd. "If you are a bachelor and you are in the women's apparel business, then obviously you are either a homosexual or a womanizer. I understand that is the perception.

"I could describe my decision to become a retailer of women's clothing in very practical terms—retailing is a good business and women shop more and spend more than men—but the fact is I got into the business by accident. My dad and mother were in the business. I wish I could give you some other answer."

But that accident has created a particular style and one that will be becoming more prevalent. Just as Wexner copies and improves upon others, others are copying and trying to improve upon him. If imitation is the sincerest form of flattery, then Wexner should feel flattered every time he takes a walk through a department store. They've taken to dividing their clothing departments into sections. They are paying greater attention to how the merchandise is displayed and they are rotating stock more frequently. And they, too, are now putting greater emphasis on creating their own brands in an attempt to boost margins and keep their customers loyal.

That is fine, but by copying Wexner, department stores are simply reacting to what he does. That means they will always be one step behind him and his ideas.

Where do the ideas come from? Wexner spends a lot of time thinking about that "because, if I understood it, I could come up with more and better ideas.

"I know the process is by observation, seeing things. I can't read things and get insights, I have to see them." But he sees them within a very special framework. He sees them through the context of being a merchant. Sure you have to understand the business—it wasn't doing Roy Raymond much good to have five stores that stocked pretty things, but lost money—but you also have to have a feel for what people will buy. And Wexner says you'll never gain that feel by merely studying the balance sheets of retailing companies. People who try, he says, are destined to fail.

"We haven't seen the shakeout of retailers yet, the real failures," Wexner says. "In the next economic downturn, you will see guys bite the dust. They are marginal now in a period of tremendous growth. When the downturn comes, I think you will see them liquidate.

"Most department stores are located in malls where they are paying incredibly low rent. They are paying $3 a square foot, and we are paying $30. They are located in the right place, and they have lots of space and they own it inexpensively. If they could rethink that space, they could be all right. But I don't think they can. History shows they can't. Macy's was the model. Here was Ed Finkelstein [Macy's chairman] who took a look at the basement of Macy's store filled with items that no one could sell and he turned it into The Cellar [an emporium filled with gourmet cooking items and expensive small appliances], and he did remarkably well. That model could have been followed by Federated, or Associated Dry Goods, Allied or the May Co. I am amazed that they didn't.

"Here is a competitor who has figured it out. If I were a competitor ten years ago, all our stores would have looked like Macy's. I would have Xeroxed them. I just don't believe they see it. Again, it is the art part of retailing. Iacocca put out a convertible and GM studies it and asks, Is it selling because it is called a K-car; because it's small; because it is a convertible; because it is red? And by the time they are done screwing around with it, three years have passed and nobody wants convertibles anymore.

"The opportunity is there, but these are not very creative people."

To underscore the point, Wexner makes an analogy between battleships (department stores) and submarines (specialty shops). "It is very difficult for a navy that is developed by battleship admirals to ever conceptualize that they may be the victim of a submarine navy. The minute they get to that, and say, 'Oh my God, the submarines are going to wipe us out. Let's start a submarine navy,' then they ask 'How do you do that?' And they have no idea. It's a lot different. Submarines are not battleships. They both go in the water, have propellers and carry guys who say 'Yes sir, and No sir, and port and starboard.' But it is a whole different point of view. The department stores are in a hell of a bind because conceptually they have trained their executives to manage and administrate. They are excellent with numbers. But, typically, they aren't merchants.

"I am a pretty good executive. I can probably run the Metropolitan Museum. But in two or three years they would be in trouble. I could run Sloan-Kettering for two or three years, but I would have a hell of a time interviewing doctors.

"You have to have a feel for what you do."

Bricks, mortar, and pizza: Defining your resources

The future of fast food may be taking shape in Omaha.

At first that may be almost impossible to understand. One's initial impression of the Godfather's Pizza chain is that it was a good idea whose time has come and gone.

Godfather's started in Omaha in 1973 as an unabashed attempt to capitalize on two American classics: pizza and the *Godfather* movies. The company even managed to combine the two in its first advertising slogan: "A pizza you can't refuse."

But while Godfather's turned in stellar performances in the mid-1970s—consistently ranking among the leaders in both sales and earnings per store, thanks to its thick crust "Chicago-style" pizzas served in a deep pan—the glory days were long gone a decade later. By then it was a struggling division within Diversifoods, a restaurant holding company probably best known for being Burger King's largest franchisee. Indeed, when Pillsbury acquired Diversifoods in 1985, it was those franchisees it wanted. Godfather's was just an afterthought.

"We justified the purchase on the basis of the Burger Kings," says J. (for John) Jeffrey Campbell, who then ran the vitally important Burger King division of Pillsbury. "We figured we would spin off Charthouse and Cork and Cleaver, Diversifood's full-service restaurants

J. JEFFREY CAMPBELL of Pillsbury

[i.e., they have waitresses], which we did. And it was an open question whether Godfather's was something we wanted to dump or not."

The reasons for dumping it were clear. The company had a dated name.[1] The locations of its restaurants were so bad that, for a while, the company used the advertising slogan "Godfather's Pizza: Find one. It is worth the trip"; and, for the longest time it looked like the company was producing more litigation, between franchisees and parent, than pizza.

As sales started to decline, franchisees began looking for more marketing and training help from the parent company, and claimed they didn't get it. Conversely, Godfather's Inc. alleged that the sales slide prompted franchisees to cut corners and to violate their franchise agreement.[2] Neither side was happy. Godfather's sales continued to fall, while overall demand for pizza soared, and lawyers were called in by both sides.

If that wasn't bad enough, competitors were taking huge bites out of Godfather's market share. Industry leader Pizza Hut, owned by PepsiCo, had come out with a deep-pan pizza, so Godfather's product was no longer unique. And spurred by the rapid climb of pizza sales, other chains were expanding rapidly. Domino's was mov-

---

1. Most pizza is bought by people aged 18 to 34 and, sad to say, not only had many of these people never seen the *Godfather* movies, a good percentage of them had never even heard of the films.

2. Not surprisingly, when sales and earnings drop at fast-food restaurants, franchisees look for ways to increase profits. An easy way to do that is to keep prices at their current levels, but switch to cheaper ingredients—less-expensive flour for the crust, lower-quality toppings for the pie. It is an understandable move, but one that is ultimately self-defeating. Using cheaper ingredients means that the quality of the pizza goes down, and eventually—when consumers discover that the product is not as good as it once was—so do sales.

ing fastest. Focusing exclusively on home delivery, the Michigan-based company quickly became the second-largest pizza chain while Godfather's slumped to fourth, behind Little Caesar (also based in Michigan, and best known for offering two pizzas for the price of one).

Given all the problems, why was Campbell—then 40 years old and one of the fastest rising executives at Pillsbury—even thinking of trying to save Godfather's? Taking on a struggling pizza chain—one with no clear identity in a marketplace dominated by far larger rivals —is not necessarily a brilliant career move. True, Campbell had made his reputation by revitalizing the listless Burger King division in the early 1980s, but for several reasons this was not Burger King redux.

First, Burger King had a clear position in consumers' minds. It was "the home of the Whopper," and the place where you could have a hamburger "your way." Godfather's was just another pizza place. Second, Burger King had a huge number of stores and an organization, one that might be sluggish but at least it was in place. Godfather's, however, was small, and franchisor and franchisees were at each other's throats. And finally, Campbell knew the hamburger business. His first job after business school had been working on the Hardee's account at the Dancer Fitzgerald Sample ad agency, and he had been in the hamburger business ever since. With the exception of having eaten Domino's pizza regularly, his experience with pizza was nonexistent.

But the novelty was part of the appeal, says Campbell. "Pizza was an interesting segment of the restaurant business, and Godfather's might prove to be an interesting way of learning about it. The pizza wasn't bad. It had been deteriorating over time [due to the switch to cheaper ingredients] but they still had a good reputation. So there was potential. There could be a lot of synergies with Pillsbury. I mean, who knows more about dough technology than Pillsbury. And Pillsbury also makes frozen pizza. So in R&D and procurement, the synergies could be dramatic.

"I would say we spent four months deliberating whether we wanted to keep Godfather's. In October 1985, we decided, let's take a shot. It is a sick business, no doubt about it, but there is probably more upside than down. They were the number-four chain, close to number three, so they were in the game. Besides, there is a huge hunk of litigation out there and until we clean it up, it would be difficult to sell this thing anyway.

"So, we said let's take a shot. Maybe we have something. At worst, we'll clean up the litigation, put training and management systems in place and standardize quality. If we do that we should be able to sell this thing in a couple of years for more than we have it on the books for. That's the worst. In the meantime, we will learn something about pizza. So if we want to take another shot at it later on, we will have educated a whole bunch of folks. So, we said, let's see what we can do."

What they did, as we will see, was nothing less than to try to redefine the rules of fast-food marketing. Campbell is using Godfather's as a laboratory, a place where he can experiment with the theories of fast-food marketing he has developed over the last 15 years.

He started by asking, "What business am I in, and what resources do I have with which to compete?"

What's new about this question? Nothing. It's Drucker 101.

But the way Campbell answered it is new. Instead of looking for the answer in his product, as many marketers do, he found the answer by looking at the broadest-possible market conditions. Campbell's conclusion is that he and Godfather's are not just in the food business. They are in the real estate business as well—and he began the experiment from there.

The experiment is not yet complete, but this much is clear: Campbell has concluded that what a restaurant sells is far less important than what it looks like, what it costs to build and how easily it can adapt to a consumer's changing needs. All marketing decisions would be made with that in mind.

Life after burgers

How did Campbell come to look at the market this way, and why was he even thinking about pizza at all? The answers stem directly from his experience with Burger King.

Campbell, who left Dancer Fitzgerald in 1971 to become Burger King's director of advertising, had moved over into operations in 1977. Pillsbury has a "fast track" program from which promising young executives are frequently transferred to various departments to get an overall view of the company. As part of that training, Campbell was given a store to run in Miami and ultimately was put in charge of New York. His ability in unifying the warring factions in the region was a key reason he was named president of Burger King in 1982, when the division was suffering.

Although the hamburger restaurants were still second to McDonald's in sales, they were producing the lowest return of any division within Pillsbury, which also owns the Steak and Ale restaurants, Green Giant vegetables and Häagen Dazs ice cream. Part of the problem was that, to a surprising extent, the fast-food business is cyclical depending on the economy, and the industry was in one of its periodic downturns. But a large part of the decline stemmed from a listlessness within Burger King. Sure, the division was a solid second in the industry, but it is hard to be thrilled about being number two. That lack of pride could be seen in a number of ways. The restaurants could have been cleaner, service faster and staff happier.

Campbell figured the best way to inspire the troops was to give them a common enemy: McDonald's. He launched "The Battle of the Burgers" advertising campaign, which said Burger King hamburgers tasted better than McDonald's. The ads received endless publicity—the only thing the business press likes writing about more than the "Cola Wars" between Coke and Pepsi is the "Hamburgers Wars" between McDonald's and Burger King—and the division responded by doubling profits within 24 months.

The turnaround convinced him that Pillsbury should begin seriously thinking about other fast-food concepts. Logical as that may seem—after all, there are only a finite number of places where you can open a hamburger stand—up to that point most franchisors didn't think about diversifying.

While a franchisee might own several Burger Kings, a Mexican place and maybe a donut shop or two, franchisors traditionally stayed with one concept. The model was McDonald's, which continued to open hundreds of outlets each year. Oh, sure, the people behind the golden arches might fiddle with the menu now and then, adding Chicken McNuggets or a prepackaged salad, but they weren't actively shopping for another restaurant chain. They stuck to what they knew best.

And what was good enough for McDonald's was good enough for the rest of the industry. For the most part, the major franchisors each stuck with a single idea.

And yet, at a January 1985 board meeting, Jeff Campbell suggested that Pillsbury think about buying another fast-food chain.

Not surprisingly, the board wanted to know why.

"It is a great question, in light of McDonald's strategy, and I suppose if you ask ten people, seven will tell you diversifying is a dumb idea. You should stick to your knitting, and all that," says Campbell. "But Burger King is in a maturing and highly competitive segment [which is growing at about 2 percent a year]. It makes sense to me to say, the less exposure you have there—not by reducing your involvement in the business, but by adding different things—the better off you are probably going to be."

The directors said Campbell's theory was fine, but they were not about to sign a blank check. They told him to come back when he had a specific acquisition in mind.

So, Campbell and his staff began looking at different restaurant "concepts," a term that has come to mean much more than just the kind of food a restaurant sells.

Back in the days when restaurant sales were booming, it was enough to be known as a place that sold steaks, or chicken or pizza. But boom times attract new competitors, each taking a piece of the market, and ultimately everyone finds growth hard to come by. When that happened, restaurant marketers began working hard to differentiate their restaurants from those of the competition.

Consider the hamburger segment for a minute. While White Castle hamburgers are sold on the basis of their low price and unique design (square burgers with five holes in them), McDonald's stresses the cleanliness of its restaurants and the consistency of its product. With the low end of the market covered, places like Fuddruckers try to go after adults by providing waitress service and liquor.

And so it goes in each segment of the industry. Some restaurant chains fry their chickens while others broil them, and the same search for differentiation held true in the pizza segment, one of the many areas Campbell considered after the board gave him permission to go shopping. "I remember looking at the emergence of Domino's; they weren't a big story yet, but you could see it coming. And I remember looking at the data on Godfather's before the illness of the business was totally apparent, and I remember saying 'God, I know why Diversifoods wants these guys. These average volumes are really good.'

"But the research was really cursory. We said acquisitions are something we want to do and we would talk about it from time to time, but then we'd go back to running Burger King. It was just on the wish list."

And suddenly, when Pillsbury acquired Diversifoods, the wish came true. Campbell had a pizza-restaurant chain if he wanted it. But did he?

Standard marketing wisdom, the kind of thing Campbell received while earning his MBA at Columbia, says that given the choice between starting a new company or turning an old one around, new is better. That way you don't have to spend time undoing what went wrong. Once a customer thinks you have problems with your product, it is very difficult—and expensive—to change that perception. It has been done, of course. Johnson & Johnson's resurrection of Tylenol is an excellent example, and by spending tens of millions of dollars to convince consumers that preshaped potato chips that fit neatly in a tennis-ball-type can are a good idea, Procter & Gamble has managed to keep Pringles on the supermarket shelf. But these are notable exceptions. It is far easier, say the textbooks, to start from scratch.

But Campbell didn't see it that way: "Godfather's had been successful before. Most of the wounds seemed self-inflicted, and the consumer—amazingly, given what they have done with their product—gave them credit for having a better-quality pizza. But the consumer also said, 'They don't have enough stores and I don't know how to find the ones they have.'

"We saw lots of opportunity for product and process improvement and creating a basic business infrastructure that wasn't there. There was potential."

Besides, despite all his enthusiasm about getting Pillsbury involved in other restaurants concepts, Campbell wasn't sure the company could compete successfully in the pizza business. Given the headstart of Pizza Hut and

Domino's, it might be too late, so why gamble tens of millions trying to create a new pizza chain? It would be far less risky to deal with what he had. Either Godfather's could be turned around, in which case the existing operation would make a formidable base, or it couldn't, and it would be sold.

"It was not a big risk; it was a little risk." That was his message to the board of directors in early 1986.

Campbell asked for $4 million and a year to stop the slide at Godfather's. "I told them if you don't like what you see after 12 months, we will sell this thing and you will probably get a lot more than you could right now, because we will have cleaned up the mess. But I added if they gave me a year, I thought we would be able to show them something." The board gave Campbell his money and the clock started ticking.

What do we do now?

At first, Campbell tried commuting periodically from Burger King's offices in Miami to Omaha, in an attempt to get things turned around at Godfather's. But he quickly realized this part-time approach would not work. "Things seemed to improve in anticipation of my arrival —[suddenly] they would have new plans they were working on—but everything seemed to stop when I left." Campbell finally grew tired of this stop-and-start approach and brought in new managers. Herman Cain, a Burger King vice president in charge of the Philadelphia region, was made president. Putting a black manager raised in Atlanta in charge of a pizza concept based in Omaha is, as they would say in Hollywood, casting against type. But Godfather's was going to need to be different to survive.

With new management in place, Campbell began by asking the most fundamental marketing questions there are: What is our strategy? What should be on our menu? How can we make money with this thing?

Answering those questions takes time. And while Cain and his staff were sorting those decisions, Campbell ordered that all advertising, which had been running $250,000 a month, be stopped. He also eliminated all price promotions such as free toppings and dollar-off coupons. Those decisions instantly cut Godfather's $6 million a year loss by more than half.

"Pizza probably has the highest percentage of cents-off and couponing in the industry," says Campbell. "You have the mom-and-pops [the small, individually owned pizzerias, which account for 60 percent of industry sales] who are fighting for survival, and then you have the infighting between them and the chains, and between the chains themselves. Everybody is scratching either for survival or market share, and the result is competition on price."

While the competition will continue indefinitely, Campbell saw no reason to spend money on promotion just to try to hold on to the market share. If Godfather's could have higher margins with fewer sales, that was fine for the time being.

And that became the strategy at first: Pare down Godfather's to its basics and then proceed from there.

Under Diversifoods, the decision had been made to broaden the menu—there were plans to add pasta and desserts—and to begin waitress service. Those ideas were put on hold. Once they were, Godfather's new managers began thinking about the number and kinds of franchises they had.

Not surprisingly, people who owned Godfather's restaurants were concerned about the turmoil at the parent company—three corporate owners within five years does not create a feeling of stability—and they were skeptical of new management. From Pillsbury's side, even a quick evaluation of the system revealed there were franchisees who were underperforming or extremely difficult to work with. Campbell and his new team used their first few months to settle the lawsuits and offer unhappy franchisees the chance to bail out. Godfather's bought out some of them, and others became franchisees of another pizza concept, most notably Pantera's, a St. Louis-based chain. Within a year, the number of Godfather's locations had been cut by nearly a third—from 900 to 650.[3]

Having finished tearing Godfather's down, it was time to start rebuilding. Campbell began by dealing with the way the restaurants were run and the pizza prepared. "They didn't have the kinds of systems that Burger King takes for granted," Campbell says. That was about to end.

Training tapes were offered to franchisees. Computer systems similar to the ones used in Burger King restaurants were made available. Instead of spending hours filling out forms that tracked inventory and personnel schedules, the computers allowed store managers to con-

3. The combination of the switch of a number of Godfather's franchisees to Pantera's, coupled with Pantera's 1987 purchase of Pizza Inn, a Dallas-based chain, made Pantera's the country's fourth-largest pizza chain. Godfather's slipped to fifth.

centrate on the quality, speed of service and cleanliness of their restaurants. And Campbell made it clear that cost cutting on ingredients would end.

All of this was fine, but really nothing more than Marketing 101. Campbell had stopped the bleeding and made the stores more efficient, but how would Godfather's grow?

I have good news. I have bad news.

He started by taking a marketer's traditional first step. He asked: What parts of the market are our competitors ignoring?

From there, conventional wisdom dictated that Campbell and company should put the new product into existing stores and add new restaurants, hoping that revenues and earnings would justify the effort.

But when you compete in a mature industry, you can't think like everyone else and hope to succeed. Campbell didn't. He looked at the equation for success backward. He said, "Number one, here are the returns I want. Two, there is the hole in the market. How can I create something that satisfies both needs?"

The answer has two parts. First, you recognize that building a restaurant to lure customers is not the only way to sell fast food. Instead of waiting for the customer to come to you, maybe you should go to them. That means, among other things, putting mini-restaurants in places where fast food is not traditionally sold.

Part two requires you to take fully into account the cost of opening a restaurant. Concern about the costs becomes so much a part of your thinking that the land needed to house the concept, and the money it takes to build it, become as important—if not more important—than the concept itself. After all, popular restaurants come and go, the land and buildings that house them last far longer.

In essence, then, Godfather's would become "an asset play." If selling pizza was the best use for the land and building, so be it. If there was more money to be made doing something else with the space, then Godfather's would change. In very large part, what Campbell is saying is that the kind of restaurant he runs within a given space is no longer the only, or even the most important, question to ask.

For a marketer—someone who, by definition, is devoted to building traffic, gathering repeat customers and, most of all, stressing the unique benefits of what he has for sale—to take this approach borders on heresy. But when PepsiCo's Pizza Hut has 5,000 restaurants, and you have just 600 and most of them are in terrible locations, heresy is called for.

For someone who frequently laughs at himself, the way Campbell describes the situation he faced, and his plans for dealing with it, is completely in character. He puts it in terms of a good news–bad news joke.

"The bad news is that Godfather's is small and fucked up," Campbell says. "The good news is the other guys are big and they may be fucked up too, or at least a little out of sync with some of the opportunities in the marketplace."

The opportunities Campbell sees are these. The pizza market is growing at 10 percent a year, but most of the sales gains are coming from home delivery—thanks almost exclusively to the spectacular rise of Domino's, which had revenues of $626 million in 1984, but more than $1.4 billion just two years later. In-store restaurant sales, the part of the industry dominated by Pizza Hut, are growing at probably 2 percent a year. Costs of putting up a full-service, Pizza Hut-type restaurant are rising far faster.

Also, focus groups revealed that consumers were growing bored. They basically had two choices when it came to eating pizza. They could bring an already-cooked pizza into their house—either by going out and picking one up, or by having a pie delivered—or they could go to a pizza parlor and eat it there. And they were almost always forced to eat pizza for dinner, given the time it takes a pizzeria to prepare a pie.

"Aren't there other choices?" pizza lovers asked the market researchers. With burgers, drive-throughs were an option, lunch was an option and even tiny hamburgers—Burger King Bundles were introduced in mid-1987—were an option. Why couldn't you do something different with pizza, too?

This unhappiness was one major finding of the market research. The other was that consumers said they would be having pizza delivered to their homes more often in coming years, as they looked for yet another way to make their lives more convenient. While home delivery already accounts for about 20 percent of the industry's $8 billion in sales, projections showed it may soon go as high as a third.

Maybe, Campbell thought, Godfather's could tap the changing market.

He started with the easy stuff: home delivery. Godfather's went to Seattle, the only place in the country where it was the market leader, and decided to take on Domino's and Pizza Hut (which was also experimenting with home delivery there) head-to-head. "Our research showed that if Godfather's pizza was available in delivery, people would prefer it to Domino's two to one.

"The appeal of Domino's is the convenience. All you do is call, and bang it is there in thirty minutes. That's what people love. It is not the price or quality. Neither of those is very exciting," says Campbell who, long before Pillsbury got into the pizza business, was eating Domino's pizza twice a week.

The Seattle experiment was vitally important. If Godfather's could succeed in home delivery, not only would it mean reversing the company's downward spiral—sales had fallen at least 10 percent in each of the three preceding years—but it would be a huge psychological boost as well. It would prove to Godfather's employees that they could compete with their far larger competitors.

To ensure success, Campbell and Cain hedged their bets. By starting in the market where Godfather's was strongest, they had the best chance of making the experiment work. You need a lot of restaurants if you are going to guarantee delivery within 30 minutes. Godfather's had them in Seattle. On-time delivery was achieved 98 percent of the time, and within months, sales in Seattle climbed 20 percent.

So far so good. The Seattle experiment got Godfather's into the fastest-growing segment of the market. The question was how else could it compete? Directly taking on Pizza Hut and its other far larger competitors would be suicide. It worked in home delivery primarily because of the size of the market. In a huge and growing market, it is usually easy for a newcomer to pick up a piece of the pie. But the rest of the pizza segment was different. Growth was slow, competition fierce.

How to compete? The answer was found in the posters Herman Cain plasters all over the Godfather's offices in a small building on the outskirts of Omaha. The signs make it clear the chain is engaged in a war. A huge target—the rings marked "winning" and "momentum," and the bull's-eye labeled "focus"—hangs behind the reception desk, and weeks of "positive sales growth" are tracked as carefully as fighter pilots monitor their kills. Nothing surprising here. Business-as-sport and business-as-war metaphors have probably been around for as long as there have been businesses, sports and war.

But Cain took it a step further. The people at Godfather's were going to be the guerrilla fighters in that war.

Now small businesses constantly use that kind of imagery. Next time you read about a small company that is about to take on IBM (or Pillsbury for that matter), you are sure to see a quote like "We are going to be guerrillas, fighting on a limited front."

But it is unusual for a big company to portray itself as an insurgent. The reason for that is simple. Small companies can make a very nice living going after the nooks and crannies of a market that big companies ignore. It is not that big companies don't want those small segments. They do. But their overhead makes it impractical for them to go after every last dollar a market has to offer.

And yet here was a big company—Pillsbury—positioning itself as a guerrilla. True, it was only saying that about one division, but that division was hardly tiny. It was a leader in the pizza segment and despite all its woes, Godfather's still had better than a quarter *billion* dollars in sales. Not exactly something you picture as a guerrilla.

The metaphor may have been unusual, but it was accurate. You could see it in the way Campbell and his staff chose to compete. If everybody was fighting for the dinner business, that was a battlefield to avoid. Godfather's would attack lunch.

The decision took advantage of the research that showed that people are looking for different ways to eat pizza. Some 80 percent of all pizza is eaten for dinner. That isn't surprising. Most people don't have more than an hour for lunch, and they are not likely to have pizza if it requires driving a couple of minutes to get to a pizza restaurant, waiting for a waitress to take their order, and then, as Campbell so artfully puts it, "spending 20 minutes sitting at a table staring into space waiting for their pie to be ready." By the time the pie arrives, more than half the lunch hour is gone.

But suppose you could get pizza within three minutes of showing up—say, by getting it by the slice? Well, then pizza for lunch becomes a whole lot more attractive. Could it be done? The funny thing was that two of Godfather's competitors had already tried variations on the concept. Campbell thought their execution was lacking. But not the concept. For more than 30 years, Jeff Campbell had thought pizza by the slice was a wonderful idea. He first realized it when he was about 10.

"Give me a slice."

As a kid growing up in New York, Campbell had bought tons of pizza by the slice. That is the way it is most often sold in New York. You walk into a pizza parlor and say, "Give me a slice." The person behind the counter cuts a wedge of a precooked pie that is sitting behind the counter, throws it in the oven, and about 90 seconds later he slaps it on a piece of wax paper that he shoves into your hands.

And by the time Campbell thought pizza by the slice might be an opportunity for Godfather's, he had more than the mom-and-pops to study to see how it might be done. Pizza Hut and Rocky Rococo had already tried it.

Pizza Hut's version? Personal Pan Pizza. A small pie —the kind tavern owners call bar pies—that Pizza Hut guaranteed you could have five minutes after a waitress took your order. It still wasn't quick. You still had to go to the Pizza Hut, wait to be seated, and then wait again for a waitress to come by. But you had to do all that anyway if you were ordering a regular pie. Personal Pan Pizza cut about 15 minutes off lunch.

No bar pies for Rocky Rococo. The Wisconsin-based chain was already selling pizza by the slice in some of its Midwestern locations, but the quality, thought Campbell, wasn't very good.

Could Godfather's combine the best elements that its competitors had to offer—the unique presentation of Pizza Hut, coupled with Rocky Rococo's idea of selling pizza by the slice—and make it taste better, too? It was certainly going to try. This was the biggest opening left in the marketplace.

It is one thing to spot an opportunity, it is another to capitalize on it quickly. Here, being a part of a large corporation proved to be an enormous help.

Folks who like to eat on the go love pizza by the slice. At the Rocky Rococo's in the Skyway Mall in Minneapolis, people would walk over, grab a slice and walk back to their office. If people were eating while walking, wouldn't they love to eat while driving? Campbell could see them pulling up to a drive-through window, ordering a slice and eating it on the way back to their home or office. After all, most burgers bought at drive-throughs are consumed that way.

What an intriguing idea. But fulfilling the fantasy would mean Godfather's would have to develop a new kind of pizza slice, one where the topping wouldn't slide off as you moved, the cheese wouldn't stretch like a rubber band when you took a bite, and the crust—especially the bottom—wouldn't get soggy and leak.

Clearly this required massive amounts of research. For an independent company, that could be not only expensive, but time consuming. But Godfather's wasn't independent, it was part of Pillsbury and who knows more about dough than Pillsbury? The prototype of the perfect traveling slice was available within weeks.[4] A name was invented—"Hot Slice"—and a sleek, wedge-shaped red box with H-O-T S-L-I-C-E printed in yellow letters superimposed on yellow and black racing stripes was created. Suddenly, Godfather's was seriously in the pizza-by-the-slice business.

"The amazing thing is that we are the first in the top

4. While understandably close-mouthed about how this was accomplished, Godfather's will say the trick was to reduce the moisture content of the pizza.

five to focus on pizza by the slice. It is the most basic idea in the world, and it hasn't been done," Campbell says. "You can have the slice within three minutes—so we are faster than Pizza Hut—ånd you can eat it the way pizza is supposed to be eaten: with your fingers. That is why God gave you fingers.

"It is a real simple idea, but they are always the best. I think this is going to provide a lot of firepower. It's an idea that can compete with delivery."

For why that is so, you need to look at the economics of the fast-food business for a minute.

Today, the cost of building a standard Burger King or McDonald's—by the time you buy the land, put up the shell and purchase the equipment—is somewhere around $1 million. And it has been rising rapidly. "At Burger King, over the last three years it went up $200,000," says Campbell. That would be okay, if revenues were keeping pace. But they are not. "The average volume over that time has hardly increased at all."

There are three reasons for that. First, there is more competition, not only for customers, but also for prime real estate. The first Burger King in a market goes in the best location, the second one, by definition, goes in the second-best location, and so on. The worse the location, the harder it is to generate sales.

The final reason for slowing sales is that the burger segment is maturing. On average, people eat at a McDonald's, Burger King, Wendy's or one of their progeny about four times a month, and that has not increased recently.

"Therefore, if you think you can afford to allow the cost of your facilities to inflate out of line with these [slowing] sales, you are going to have a big problem," Campbell says. "You have to respond to this situation by getting more creative. You have to play the game differently."

And Godfather's is Campbell's first attempt to do that.

Think about the two areas where it appears that Godfather's has the best shot: home delivery and HOT SLICE. Neither takes a lot of capital investment. You can do home delivery out of existing stores, and a store that specializes in selling Hot Slices doesn't require much money. Yes, you need to buy pizza-making equipment, but no, you don't need a large facility. You don't need room for tables and chairs because you are not going to provide waitress service. People are going to walk up, order the slice and leave. You can probably open a facility in 350 square feet as opposed to the 3,500 square feet needed for a standard Burger King or McDonald's.

Look what that does to the economics of the fast-food business. Let's say it costs $1 million to open a Burger King next year, and let's put that mythical Burger King in a good location, one that will generate $1 million in sales. The result? Your $1 million investment yields $1 million in revenues.

But suppose you were to spend that $1 million on opening Hot Slice units instead. They cost about $200,000 each, so you can open five for $1 million. But a Hot Slice unit, on average, should yield $250,000 in revenues. So that $1 million investment produces $1.25 million in sales. Assuming margins at Burger King and Hot Slice are the same—and they are—that means the same $1 million will produce a return *that is 25 percent greater*.

That kind of increase is enough to get Campbell to rethink everything he has learned about the fast-food business.

Hold that knee

"The reaction our knee wants to make, given our experience over the last 20 years, is to define all the opportunities Godfather's has in terms of freestanding restaurants that look just like existing Burger Kings," Campbell says. "Well, let's just think twice about that. We have the flexibility to define where we want to be. Freestanding units, like we have, may be part of it, but there are other avenues of distribution that we may have a tendency to walk past that are really in tune with where customers are going.

"Let's assume Americans want to eat a lot of pizza, and the consumption data that we see says there is more real growth over the next ten years in pizza than there is in burgers. But how people consume that pizza may be changing."

Those changes, Campbell believes, could work to Godfather's advantage. It is small enough to be able to respond to the evolving market. Godfather's doesn't have 5,000 restaurants as Pizza Hut does, and unlike Domino's it has the capability to do more than just deliver pizza. "We have a lot of flexibility, and as the market changes, we might just catch the wave," Campbell says. "If consumers want Hot Slice, we can do that. If they want delivery, we can do that. If they want to pick up a pizza at the supermarket and finish it at home, well, we can do that too. There is unlimited potential."

But unlimited potential could mean unlimited problems. If you try to do too many things, there is no focus. Domino's means home delivery. Pizza Hut is where you go when you want to sit down and eat a pie. But if Godfather's tries to be all things to all people, no one will know what it stands for, or when to buy its products.

Campbell concedes the point, but says it is too early to worry about it. "We don't have to do everything. We can pick from a selection of strategies. It's really like sitting out there on a surf board with a big set about to come through. You are not sure which of them you are going to take, but you know each of them is probably pretty good."

Which waves he rides will be determined by consumers. "I think we pretty much have to react to you. We have to convince you we have a great-tasting pizza. Once we do, you tell us how you want to get it. Do you want to eat in, take it out, or have it delivered to your home? We see the beginnings of preprepped pizzas that you finish at home. Having only 600 restaurants—which is not small, but it is not huge—we are able to define the market first. But before we define ourselves in the traditional quick-service-restaurant mode, let's think twice about this son of a bitch."

And that thinking goes beyond how to sell pizza in a form that is most convenient for consumers. It always includes a calculated look at how to make the most money doing it.

Companies with a lot of fixed assets, specifically buildings, have to adjust to a changing market the best they can. Take a restaurant chain: As the market starts to change, they can first fiddle with the menu. That's easy, and equally important, inexpensive. But if that doesn't work, they have some potentially expensive decisions to make. While they'd love to chase an evolving market, they can't abandon all the money they have in existing facilities.

For example, Domino's may decide tomorrow it wants to be a full-service restaurant chain, but if it does, what does it do with the 4,000 relatively tiny home-delivery outlets it has nationwide?

Godfather's isn't shackled. If it wants to specialize in Hot Slice, it doesn't have to worry about all the dead space it has in existing restaurants. There just aren't that many restaurants. It can decide tomorrow that every new restaurant will be a tiny one devoted to Hot Slice.

And think for a minute about the possibilities having smaller facilities gives you. You can put them in places where you never could before; places like shopping malls. Only 25 percent or so of the nation's malls have fast-food outlets, and the reason is simple. The cost of renting mall space—roughly $30 a square foot—can be prohibitive. For the typical Burger King or McDonald's it would come to better than $1 million a year.

But paying $30 a square foot for just *300* square feet becomes a much more attractive proposition. "You can go into a mall, rent some space and, with equipment, the whole thing costs you $150,000 to $175,000—and you get $200,000 out of it. It could be decent," Campbell says with a smile. And if you can plug a Hot Slice in a mall, you could put it in other places where there is not a lot of room: museums, airports, train stations. Says Campbell: "There are a lot of ways to skin a cat.

"What will probably end up happening at all our restaurants is that we will break our facilities down into three or four investment levels. Maybe everything from a 300-square-feet Hot Slice unit to a full-sized Burger King. And we will target sales levels so that we get a great return on each. But in each market, you will have a mix of facilities. One size will not fit all.

"Capital is [now] such a huge piece of this industry that you can't position a concept without defining what the facility is," Campbell adds. "So whether it is Oriental[5] or Italian, or some other speculative venture, you just can't tell me what the product is and how you are going to sell it to consumers. I also want to understand what that physical thing that sells it is going to look like, and if there is more than one kind of facility, I want to understand how they all fit together and what the rate of return is going to be. The real estate facility strategy is now as much a part of the positioning of the concept as the advertising, promotion and menu.

"And that is the way we are doing our development planning now. It isn't the way we did it four years ago. Then we didn't worry about it. We said let's have one or two types of buildings and shove them out there. Well, you can't do that any more. When there is steady inflation in the cost of land, buildings and equipment, unless you are in an era where your new store volumes are growing at the same or a greater rate, it is going to affect your returns, and you are supposed to adjust. At least," Campbell says with a laugh, "that is what they taught me. You don't keep marching."

5. Pillsbury is also experimenting with a chain of Oriental fast-food restaurants called Quick Wok.

What you do is look for another way of going forward. "Again, as the burger segment matures, you can either say, 'It's maturing, and I will slow my rate of growth,' or you can say, 'It is maturing, and I will slow my rate of traditional growth—but I will look for untraditional opportunities out there that may keep me growing at the same rate. It just will look a little different.' "

"The most boring places in the world"

And not only will looking different help increase the rate of return, it will also help keep consumers interested in your restaurants, Campbell believes.

"I was out in Los Angeles recently, toying with an idea I have for a new concept, and I must have sat through four or five focus groups every day, and I came back saying I am going to have every guy on our team do this for two days every year, because this is truth serum."

Now it seems surprising that a premier marketer would become charged up about sitting in on focus groups. After all, the secret to marketing is finding out what people want. So why wasn't Campbell sitting in on these sessions all along?

"Let me get on my soapbox for a minute," Campbell replies. "In corporate America, we are our own worst enemy, and bureaucracy is the tendency of the age, and maybe every other age. The bigger you get, the more insulated you tend to become, and the less likely it is that you are ever going to see a customer. And our excuses for this are pretty lame. We are very busy. We have to go to meetings. Have to read the numbers." And, in doing so, you lose touch with the marketplace.

So, to understand what is going on, Campbell sat in on focus groups and talked to consumers. The results to someone who has spent his entire working life in the fast-food business can be amazingly disheartening.

"You go out and you ain't going to blow smoke up anyone's ass. People have an absolute-bullshit detector. And you find out that what you think is exciting, triggers a big yawn. They tell you, 'Burger King, McDonald's, I can't tell the difference.'

"What do you mean you can't tell the difference? I spend my life on that!

"But even worse, they tell you [that fast-food restaurants] are the most boring places in the world.

"And that is what I worry about," says Campbell. "I can remember going to a Howard Johnson on a trip with my parents in 1957, and my father bitching about the service, which I remember was bad. And Howard Johnson had it all to themselves then. And they blew it.

"Burger King, McDonald's, Wendy's—and let's forget the little differences between us right now—the world has been our oyster for 25 years. And what really scares me when I hear consumers talk, is that we have educated a couple of generations on convenience food, but they want more. They can get more. In a capitalistic system, desire generally produces options. You can be fickle. There is always going to be someone new tomorrow."

And as those new concepts come along "we begin to look a little like an updated version of Howard Johnson." Why? Because marketers have become too busy to listen to their market. And as Campbell discovered, to his chagrin, there is a lot to listen to.

"Consumers say, 'You guys used to be fast service but

now you are kind of becoming a cliché for don't-give-a-shit service. You're kind of getting to be plastic, plastic, plastic. You were built that way, because speed and consistency is all you could offer. But now, you are kind of boring.'

"And here comes a new guy, and he is doing it in a different way and it feels pretty good. And now I start to worry about having a boredom factor setting in when there are lots of other alternatives out there, and I'm sitting on a huge chunk of invested capital.

"There are cases of companies that have gone away. Howard Johnson is a perfect example."

The question to Campbell is how to ensure that doesn't happen. And not surprisingly for someone who has a masters in European history to go with his MBA, Campbell looks to the past to deal with the future.

"What would have happened back in 1965[6] if Howard Johnson had said—and remember, everybody: McDonald's, KFC, us, was real small back then—let's buy one of these concepts. In fact, let's buy beef and chicken, that way we will hedge our commodity bets. Where would they be today? They'd be bigger than PepsiCo. But they were just watching the numbers. The last quarter was pretty good. A risk like that? We are not going to get an immediate return.

"So those are the things you worry about. Howard Johnson didn't have any security. What can you count on?

"In truth, you count on people eating, and they are not always going to prepare the food themselves. There al-

6. Back in 1965, as we have seen, Howard Johnson's sales were greater than McDonald's, Burger King's and Kentucky Fried Chicken's *combined*.

ways were restaurants, there always will be. It is just a matter of whose."

And the secret to keeping people coming to yours, says Campbell, is to recognize that tastes change. People who go out for burgers today may become vegetarians tomorrow. But that does not have to be a problem, if you can spot those shifts early. And there is no better way of doing that than simply talking to the people you are courting, and recognizing that what worked yesterday may not work tomorrow.

"If you start with thinking flexibly, keeping your eyes open to what is next and managing your real estate, you can do okay. You can ride each successive wave of what the consumer wants.

"Let's go five or six years out and see what could happen," Campbell says, by way of example. "Suppose, overnight, they discover hamburgers cause cancer. McDonald's owns all that property and they say, 'We are going to sell it and you franchisees are out of luck.' Can you imagine the litigation? Whoo!

"That is something I think about with Burger King. What do we do if that happens? Okay, first, in our system the franchisees own more property than we do, so we are in a better position. But second, if we had another concept to give them—say we offer to swap them a Godfather's for a Burger King—it will become a more manageable deal.

"Most of the people running businesses don't want to think about these things. They want to think about what promotion they are running next quarter. But you have to think about them."

You have to, not because it is likely that we will find

out someday that hamburgers do cause cancer, but because people are growing bored more quickly than ever before, and you have to be prepared to adjust.

"Consumers tell you: 'I want to see something new. Some different kind of food. Not anything radical, although there is some interesting ethnic food out there, but I am looking to experiment a little bit. Don't bore me. I want to have some fun.'

"In the full-service restaurant, the boredom factor is much more intense. I was having dinner in Dallas at the Key West Grill, the newest Steak and Ale concept, and people were hanging off the walls. The place is great fun. The whole thing is a Key West bar, a Hemingway-type thing. Five years from now that will be gone. That was fun. I don't want to go there anymore. Well, then if you are smart you turn the Key West Grill into Mikhail Gorbachev's Balalaika Palace. There, that's a new idea, let's go there.

"As we look across all the restaurants we have, the question is how many different types of building shells should we have? Maybe there are only four that are common to all. And if we do the real estate procurement right, and we have the building situation right, the worst that should ever happen is that we remodel from concept X to concept Y. The major part of the investment [and land and buildings] will remain sound as the dollar."

In reality, what Campbell has done in plotting the strategy of all of Pillsbury's restaurants[7] is to ask the most basic questions of all: What business am I really in, and what resources do I have with which to compete?

7. Campbell, an executive vice president at Pillsbury, was named to the newly created position of chairman of its restaurant group in 1987.

The business answer is simple: Campbell is in the restaurant business, broadly defined. The fact that Burger King offers Whoppers today does not necessarily mean that it has to offer Whoppers tomorrow.

As for the resources at his command, Campbell understands that it is more than staff, advertising and buildings that house Burger King, Godfather's, and the other Pillsbury restaurants, and he also understands that how those assets are used today will not be the way they are used tomorrow.

These realizations are far from new. If you have an asset—the space occupied by the Key West Grill, for example—that stops producing the kinds of returns you want, you change it. Financial types would describe this kind of thinking as an asset play, and Campbell says this approach to the market, even among restaurants, is not new.

"At McDonald's, Harry Sanborn [chief financial officer during McDonald's formative years] came up with a genius stroke. He went out and told bankers, who didn't understand what Ray Kroc was talking about, McDonald's was a real estate company. He said, 'We are investing in real estate and the best use of it right now is burgers.' This is the biggest idea in the industry, as far as I am concerned.

"McDonald's doesn't think about it that way any more, but that is exactly the way we are thinking about it with the Pillsbury restaurant group. We haven't developed our thinking all the way yet, but that is how we see it."

So in the best of all possible worlds, Godfather's Pizza becomes a successful addition to the Pillsbury restaurant group. In the worst of all possible worlds, it becomes a possible replacement, or at least partial substitute, for Burger King.

The building will remain the same, only the kind of food will change.

8 Conclusion: Tailfins will be back

The next time you are wandering through the parking lot of a shopping mall searching for your car, or find yourself on a long drive, take a look at the cars around you. You'll notice that half of them look like Honda Accords. They slope down in front. Their backs are squared off, and from the side they look like a wedge of cheese.

Part of the reason for this is that imitation, often, *is* the sincerest form of flattery. Whether the dollar is weak or strong, Hondas continue to appeal to Americans, and maybe, the folks in Detroit figure, if they copy the outward appearance of a Honda, some of its appeal will rub off.

But there is another reason why most new cars look alike. Auto companies today—both here and overseas—have access to the same bright MBAs, their market research departments are more or less equal, and the competitive nature of the industry makes it certain that they have taken apart their rivals' cars and have examined every component within days of introduction. Starting from this equal footing, with more or less the same resources, it is not surprising they reach the same conclusions about what consumers want. And today, they have concluded, most people want cars that look like a Honda Accord.

The Honda Accord example is a good metaphor for modern marketing. To understand why that is so, it is important to back up just a bit.

In times of plenty, strange as it may seem, marketing is just not that important. When people have money burning holes in their pockets, you don't need to be a marketing master to get them to part with it. Demand will outstrip supply, and almost anything you do will lead to higher sales.

In that kind of environment—be it caused by pent-up demand that broke out following the end of World War II, or a sudden influx of working women creating dual-income families—you don't need marketers running your companies. You don't have to worry about whether the cash register is going to ring. It will.

But ironically, good times cause exactly the wrong people to be promoted. How often do you read of a company, which has reported booming sales while the economy is humming along, moving marketing executives to the fore? It happens all the time, in companies big and small. "Old Charlie down in marketing must be doing a heck of a job," people say when a company notches record sales—which in reality have grown only as fast as the economy as a whole. And Charlie gets promoted, even though he really hasn't done anything except ride a rising economic tide.

Instead of promoting marketers when times are good, companies should be attempting to increase earnings on those rising sales. It is in times of plenty that they should be turning to administrative and finance people, instead of waiting for the inevitable downturn to "cut fat" and "streamline production." As Thomas Watson, the man who made IBM IBM, noted: Companies most often get into trouble, not when times are bad, but when they are good.

But unfortunately, few people see it this way. If things were good yesterday, and are good today, then surely they will be good forever, is their attitude. And by the time they discover that trees don't grow to the sky, their companies are in trouble. What is their first move to turn things around? They put finance people in charge. That is fine—but only as a short-term measure.

Just as you don't want to have marketing people in charge when times are good, you don't want to have finance people at the helm in times of zero or slow growth.

You may find that counterintuitive, but it really does make sense. Just look around. Today the systems put in place to "maximize returns" no longer yield an edge. Everyone has them. And everyone has access to the same kind of research and the same bright MBAs and consultants. The result is that everyone is producing cars that look like the Honda Accord. Since everyone is following the same logic, no one has a competitive edge.

In a booming economy that wouldn't matter. Companies would be happy to hold on to market share, content in the knowledge that the economy would cause their sales and earnings to increase.

But the economy isn't booming. And faced with zero or little growth, financial and professional managers looking for an edge do what they do best: They test extensively and conduct in-depth focus groups and market research. There is nothing wrong with that. But as Leslie Wexner, chairman of The Limited, pointed out, focus groups will never yield anything dramatically new. They can tell you in a vague sort of way what is wrong with your product ("I don't know, all hamburger places are becoming kind of boring"), but they aren't very helpful in telling you what to do about it ("I want some excitement; I want to try something new").

Faced with this situation, companies run by financial and administrative types—as most now are, according to surveys by *Forbes* and *Business Week*—will do what they are comfortable with. They'll make small, incremental improvements to their products. And slowly their cars begin to look more and more like Honda Accords.

Wizards of Oz need not apply

In a marketplace where the pie isn't getting any bigger, if you tend to act like everyone else, you won't score any smashing successes. In fact, all you'll do is labor long and hard to stay in place—if you're lucky. Consider General Motors, which is guilty of the Honda Accord syndrome. For all the billions it has spent in recent years "to remain competitive," it has steadily lost market share. Why? Well, one way to answer that question is to ask another. When was the last time GM produced a car as distinctive as its Corvette or Firebird of old?

In today's environment, people who are wizards when it comes to manipulating spreadsheets are not what is needed. Required are corporate leaders who can separate their companies from the pack. In short, today's companies need marketers, or better yet, marketing masters.

What does it take to be a marketing star? The common thread that runs through the stories presented here is this: Each successful marketer had good financial and administrative skills. But that, as we have seen, should now be taken as a given. *What truly makes them stand out is that they have a thorough understanding of their customers and they act on that "feel," once they see or sense an opportunity. They act without laboring over research reports and focus-group summaries, the traditional tools of the trade. They use those tools to confirm their ideas (or hunches), not to provide insights or inspiration.*

And their ideas or hunches aren't revolutionary, in the sense that they are totally unexpected. They are—99.99 times out of a hundred—improvements on what has come before. Improvements, not in the sense an MBA would use the term—more efficient production processes or a less expensive formula—but real improvements. Making a product better, having it become more responsive to a customer's need.

That point needs to be underlined. The natural reaction most of us would have if we were asked to describe what makes stellar marketers would be to say they have the ability to create something that has never existed before, things like the Polaroid camera, or even Silly Putty.

But none of the people we have met here did that. They didn't create anything. Advertising man David Bell is probably the most graphic example of that. He didn't invent the concept of advertising; heck, he didn't even invent the idea of using a bull as Merrill Lynch's corporate symbol. All of that existed before. Bell simply said: With the bull, Merrill Lynch has one of the best-known advertising symbols the world has ever seen. How can we take advantage of that?

And so it went with each man we met. Lemon-lime sodas existed before Slice. Roger Enrico just found a way to make them taste better and shouted about his discovery with $30 million a year in advertising. There have been phone books for virtually as long as there have been phones. Ron Jennings just targeted them to a new audience.

Again, to be a successful marketer, you don't have to invent the wheel, just a new use for it, and you must do it quickly. In a marketing environment where the resources are just about equal across the board, you don't have time to study an issue to death. If you do, someone else will beat you to the consumer's wallet.

This willingness to act will become more important in coming years. As the marketplace becomes more crowded, you are going to have to stand out in order to succeed. A smarter, more experienced consumer will demand that your product be different. If we want to extend the car analogy that we started with for a bit, you will have to place tailfins on all those Honda Accord-type cars.

But what kind of tailfins should you add? To answer that question, marketers must keep in mind three things:

First, they are no longer marketing in the days of *Ozzie and Harriet,* when there was a huge mass market. The mass market grows smaller by the day. Consumers' needs have changed.

The second point follows the first. Marketers will have to produce products to satisfy those changing needs. We have seen two excellent strategies for doing that.

The first calls for making your product more convenient than anyone else's. Pillsbury is not only doing this through home delivery of pizza—the ultimate form of convenience—but also by selling pizza by the slice. That makes it possible to have pizza at lunch, which is a more convenient time for some, and also allows customers to purchase it at a more convenient place: the drive-through window.

Convenience also means making buying easier. The Limited succeeded with Victoria's Secret because it made shopping for lingerie more convenient by providing a much wider selection than ever before.

The second way of meeting changing needs is by designing a product that fits in with the way people live today. Slice has done that effectively. Health-conscious people—who, paradoxically, insist on having soft drinks of dubious nutritional value—feel better about consuming a soft drink containing juice.

The last part of the three-part strategy requires marketers to effectively explain to consumers that they have met their needs. They need to produce commericals that get attention.

To cut through the clutter, expect to see an increased use of corporate symbols, like the Merrill Lynch bull, in coming years. The symbols will be used to underscore the commercial's message—you know the bull stands for Merrill Lynch—and as a way of making the commercial stand out.

None of this is very hard. It just requires marketers to act on it. The good ones have already started.

Acknowledgments

I am no longer jealous of the fact that Lawrence J. Nagy, a classmate of mine at law school, is smarter than I am. What I can't stand is that he is funnier.

It was Larry who asked, after listening to a colleague explain about the endless breakfast, lunch and dinner meetings it took him to put together a book deal: "Is it written somewhere that you can't talk about a book project unless you have silverware in your hand?"

It is thanks to people like Larry that my waistline has remained intact. When you deal with professionals, it doesn't take a whole lot of time—or meetings that require silverware—to get things done.

For that I have many people to thank. First and foremost is Harriet Rubin. She, more than anyone else, is responsible for the book's shape. The mistakes are mine. The clever ideas are hers. The others at Harper & Row—most notably John Michel and Janet Coleman—who managed to see this through from idea to execution have earned my undying admiration.

Certainly the executives at each and every company profiled here have to be singled out. All gave unstintingly of their time, made sure I got all the backup materials I needed and kept their sense of humor when I called back for the fourth or fifth time with "just a couple more questions."

For their time and insights I also want to thank Alan J. Zakon, chairman of the Boston Consulting Group, and Laurel Cutler, vice chairman of Leber Katz/Foote Cone Belding. There are certainly no smarter people anywhere when it comes to marketing.

The people at the Goldhirsh Group—specifically Bernie Goldhirsh—and at *Inc.*—George Gendron, Bo Burlingham, Sara Noble and Michael Hopkins—understood and never complained about how long it takes to put a book together.

And finally, thanks to Anne Christine Peck, Peter and Shannon for their support, which made writing this much easier. (I want to offer a special thanks to Peter, who upon occasion was willing to stop playing "Spaceyators" so that I could use the computer to write.)

Index

Abdul-Jabbar, Kareem, 88
Add-ons, 78
Advertising, 15–40, 104
  "The Battle of the Burgers," 174
  bull in, 15–18, 20, 26–28, 31, 37, 38, 40
  children and, 89
  docudramas, 18–19, 22–23
  expenditures for, 21–22
  financial-service, 20–21
  Godfather's Pizza, 170, 179
  market changes and, 124
  purpose of, 160
  in Silver Pages, 129, 131, 136
  Slice, 57–65, 67
  Southwestern Bell, 112, 131–33
  spot market, 63
  Wexner's views on, 139, 158–61
  Worlds of Wonder and, 78, 100–2
  in Yellow Pages, 116
Adweek, 38
Age, 6, 8–9, 11, 121
Alchemy II, 79, 94
American Express, 20
Americtech, 111
Appleman, William, 22
Apple Slice, 68, 70
Applied Data Research, 111
AT&T, 109–11, 115, 117–19, 134

Baby-boomers, 5–11
Bache Halsey, 20
Bangles, 88
"Battle of the Burgers, The," 174
Bell, Alexander Graham, 112
Bell, David, 22–23, 25–37, 40, 206
Bell Atlantic, 111, 117

Bell of Pennsylvania, 117
BellSouth, 111
Berra, Yogi, 140
Boredom, customer, 161
Bottlers, 62–64, 67–68
Bozell Jacobs Kenyon & Eckhardt (BJK&E), 22–40
Brand loyalty, 163
Brazil, 51
Bryant, Lane, 143
Burger King, 7, 58, 168, 171, 173–76, 180, 183, 189, 190, 196, 197n, 200, 201
Burson-Marsteller, 39
Business Week, 205
Byte Shops, 111

Cabbage Patch, 90
Caffeine-free colas, 51, 65, 67
Cain, Herman, 178–79, 184, 185
Campbell, J. Jeffrey, 168, 171–84, 186–200
Cars, look-alike, 202–5
Cash Management Account, 36
Cellar, The, 166
Change, 1–11
Cherry Coke, 68–70
Cherry Cola Slice, 68–70
Cherry Pepsi, 68
Chiat/Day, 100
Children
  advertising and, 89
  market testing and, 92–97
  social changes and, 88–94
Chuck E. Cheese (pizza parlor), 80
Clothing. *See* Lingerie business; The Limited; Victoria's Secret

Coca-Cola, 41, 43
Coffee, 10
Coke, 10, 40, 45–46, 51, 67, 71–73
Cola Wars, 174
Coleco, 80
Commercial Funding, 111
Commercials. *See* Advertising
Competition, 20, 78–79
  in fast food industry, 174, 177–79,
    181–86
  international, 3–5
  phone books and, 110, 118, 130–31
  product introduction and, 60–62
  soft drinks and, 51–52, 60–62, 67
Computer systems, 180–81
Consumers. *See also* Customers
  age of, 121
  changes in, 5–11, 207
  diversity of, 124
  of fast food, 181–84, 198, 199
  health concerns of, 48–49
  importance of understanding, 206
Convenience, 182–85, 207–8
Country Jamboree, 80, 82
Courtney's, 146, 149
Creative process, 139–40
Creativity, types of, 145, 155–56
Credit cards, 136
Customers, 137, 139, 153, 155–56,
    161. *See also* Consumers

Dancer Fitzgerald Sample (DFS), 24,
    35, 36, 171, 173
Dart & Kraft, 113
Dart Drug, 113
Dean Witter, 20
Department stores, 6–7, 9–10, 148,
    149, 159, 163–64, 166
Diet Cherry Coke, 68
Diet Coke, 46, 63, 64
Diet colas, 51
Diet Pepsi, 63
Diet Rite Cola, 67n
Direct-mail marketers, 125
Direct marketers, 10
Disney World, 80, 82
Distribution of soft drinks, 62–63
Diversifoods, 168, 170, 176, 179
Docudramas, 18–19, 22–23

Domino's, 9, 170–71, 176, 178, 183,
    184, 191–93
Doritos, 67

Education, 6, 8–9
E.F. Hutton, 21
Elderly, the. *See* Senior citizens
Electronic delivery systems, 114
Electronic games, 79–80
Elgort, Robert, 37n
Emotions, 95, 97
Enrico, Roger, 43, 207. *See also* Slice

Falcon, Leonard, 99n
Fantasy, Victoria's Secret and, 140,
    153–54, 161–62
Fast food, 168–201. *See also specific
    chains*
  competition in, 174, 177–79, 181–
    86
  diversification and, 174–75
  economics of, 190–91
  real estate and, 173, 190, 193–94
Federal Express, 155
Finkelstein, Ed, 166
First Boston, 17
Floyd, Raymond, 131–32
Focus groups, 183, 204–5
Forbes, 112–13, 205
Forenza line, 157, 158, 163
Frito-Lay, 44, 56, 67
Fuddruckers, 176

General Foods, 10
General Motors (GM), 205
Gibson, Verna, 137, 139, 157, 159
Godfather's Pizza, 168–73, 176–93,
    200–1
  advertising of, 170, 179
  as Campbell's laboratory, 172–73
  computer systems of, 180–81
  Hot Slice of, 188–91, 193
  management changes at, 178–79
  menu diversification at, 179–80
  origin of idea for, 168
  sales decline of, 170
  Seattle experiment of, 184
Goizueta, Roberto, 45–46, 72
Grant, Cary, 28–29

Grey Advertising, 24
Groups, Wexner's views on, 139, 155
Guilt, parental, 89

Health concerns of consumers, 48–49
Health consciousness, 208
Hi-C, 47, 72
Home delivery, 182–85, 208
Honda Accord, 202–5
Hope, Bob, 132–33
Hot Slice, 188–91, 193
Houseman, John, 21
Howard Johnson, 7, 10, 155, 196–97
Hunter's Run brand, 157

Iacocca, Lee, 160, 167
Imagination, 100, 145
Imitation, 145
Inflation, 4, 5
Innovation, 145–46, 155–56
ITT, 144

Jackson, Michael, 58, 63
Japan, 3, 44, 71–72
Jennings, Ron, 108–9, 113, 119–31, 133–36, 207
Johnson & Johnson, 177
Juice, in soft drinks, 44–45, 47–48
Justice Department, U.S., 110
J.G. Hook, 142, 150
J. Walter Thompson, 58–62

Kensington Datacom, 111
Kentucky Fried Chicken, 7, 44, 197n
Key West Grill, 199
King, Carole, 140
Kingsborough, Don, 75, 77–105
Knocking it off, 156–57
Kodak, 3, 59
Kraft, 113
Kroc, Ray, 142, 200

Labels, 162–63
Land's End, 125
Lazer Tag, 77, 82–92, 96–105
  cost of, 82–83, 88–89
  criticism of, 99–100
  outdoors use of, 83

Lazer Tag *(cont.)*
  public relations for, 86–88
  sales for, 103
  StarLyte and, 85, 88, 98, 102
  Starsensor and, 85
  teenage market for, 84–85, 101
Lazer Tag Academy, 104
Lemon-lime soft drinks. *See* Seven-Up; Slice
Leonardo da Vinci, 145
Lerner Store, 160
Licensing arrangements, 78
Like, 51, 67n
Limited Express, 160
Lingerie business, 146–55. *See also* Victoria's Secret
Lippert, Barbara, 38
Lite Beer, 3
Little, Arthur D., 46
Little Caesar, 171
L.L. Bean, 125
Louganis, Greg, 88
Love Story (movie), 152

McDonald's, 7, 58, 155, 174–76, 189, 196–98
McGovern, Maureen, 37n
Macgraw, Ali, 152
Macy's, 166
Mail-order catalogs, 10, 161–62
Marketing, 1–11
Marketing stars, 205–8
Market research (surveys), 137, 139, 155–56, 158, 186, 188
Marlboro, 2–3
Mass market, 6–9, 124
Mass Industries, 163
Matalish, Ray, 129–30
Mattel, 80
"Me" generation, 92
Mergers and acquisitions, 113
Merrill Lynch, 12–40, 206, 208
Middle class, disappearance of, 8
Milton Bradley, 80
Minute Maid (orange soda), 67
Mr. Blandings Builds His Dream House (movie), 28–29
Montgomery Ward, 7, 9
Morita, Akio, 139, 140

Murphy, James E., 12, 14–16, 19–21, 23–26, 32, 39, 40

Names, product, 55–59
National Association of Area Agencies on Aging (NAAAA), 122–23, 126–28
New-Coke debacle, 71–73
New Jersey Bell, 110, 117
New York Toy Fair, 98, 99
New York Yellow Pages, 119
NYNEX, 111, 119

Ogilvy & Mather (O&M), 16, 17, 27
Older Americans Act (1965), 122–23
Orange Crush, 66
Orange Slice, 65–67, 69–70
Outback Red, 157, 163

Pacific Telesis, 110, 111, 117–18
Packaging, 156–57
Pantera's, 180
Parent-child relations, 88–90
Parsons, Al C., 114
Peebler, Chuck, 33
Penney, J.C., 9
PepsiCo, 2, 10, 11, 40, 41, 43–73, 182. *See also* Slice
Pepsi-Cola, 44
Pepsi Free, 65, 67, 68
Pepsi Light, 70
Personal Pan Pizza, 187
Peter Principle, 97
Philip Morris (PM), 2, 22, 51–52
Phone books, 106–10, 112–36, 207. *See also* Silver Pages
  cost of, 115–17
  as mature business, 114
  profitability of, 115, 133–34
  specialty, 122
  Yellow Pages, 109, 114–17, 119
Picasso, Pablo, 139
Pillsbury, 168–201, 208. *See also* Burger King; Godfather's Pizza
  Diversifoods acquired by, 168, 170, 177
  fast track program of, 173–74

Pillsbury *(cont.)*
  Godfather's Pizza's synergy with, 172
  as guerrilla, 185–86
Pizza, 168–73. *See also* Domino's; Godfather's Pizza; Pizza Hut
  growth in market for, 182–83
  home delivery of, 182–85, 208
  new ways to eat, 186
  by the slice, 187–88
  time requirements and, 186–89
Pizza Hut, 44, 170, 177–78, 182–84, 187–89, 191–92
Polaroid, 3
Pong, 79
Pope, Robert, 120–21
Pornography, 162
Primerica, 21
Pringles, 177
Procter & Gamble, 2, 22, 177
Product differences, 41–74, 207. *See also* Slice; Soft drinks
  credibility issues and, 48–49
  importance of, 43–44
  names and, 55–59
Product success, 75–105. *See also* Lazer Tag; Worlds of Wonder
Prudential Bache, 22–24
Prudential Insurance, 20
Public relations, 78, 86–88, 104
Public-utility commissions, 110

Quality, 91
Quick Wok, 194*n*

Rago, Paul, 75, 77, 82–84, 97
Rainbow brands, 65–71
Raymond, Roy, 147–51, 166
Real estate, fast food and, 173, 190, 193–94
Regan, Donald, 14, 17
Regional Bell, operating companies, (RBOCs), 110–12
Resources, definition of, 168–201
Restaurant "concepts," 175–76
Restaurants. *See also* Fast food
  start up costs for, 181–82
Retail displays, 78
Rocky Rococo, 187, 188

Sanborn, Harry, 200
Schreyer, William, 33
Schwab, Charles, 20
Sculley, John, 43, 46
Sears, 7, 9, 20
Senior citizens, 122–25, 128, 129. *See also* Silver Pages
Service businesses, 14–15, 125
7-Eleven, 9
Seven-Up, 3, 11, 41, 43, 45, 52, 61–63
Seven-Up Co., 51–55
Sex, customer fantasies and, 161–62
Shasta, 66
Shearson, 20, 22
Shopping malls, 160–61, 164, 202
Sierra Spring Water Co., 56, 57
Silver Pages, 11, 120–36
    advertising in, 136
    AT&T breakup and, 134
    contents of, 129
    cooperation of area agencies on aging and, 126–27, 129–30
    cost of advertising in, 129
    inducements for use of, 136
    leaks and, 131
    origin of idea for, 120–22
    profits from, 133–34
Slice, 11, 41, 45–72, 208
    advertising of, 57–65, 67
    contents of, 49n
    cost of, 48, 50
    development of, 43–55
    distribution of, 62–63
    endorsement of, 50–51
    health issues and, 48–50
    introduction of, 53–55
    naming of, 55–59
    new Coke and, 71–73
    rainbow brands of, 65–71
    test markets of, 64–65
Smith Barney, 21
Smith Marketing, 87–88
Social change, 88–94
Soft drinks, 10–11, 207, 208. *See also specific soft drinks*
    all-natural, 49
    bottlers of, 62–64, 67–68
    competition and, 51–52, 60–62, 67

Soft drinks *(cont.)*
    credibility of healthiness of, 48–50
    kind of juice in, 47–48
    market testing of, 66, 69, 72, 73
    percentage of juice in, 47, 65, 66
    product difference and, 41–74
    rainbow brands of, 65–71
    taxes and, 44–45
    test markets for, 46, 53, 54
Southwestern Bell, 2, 11, 106–36, 131. *See also* Silver Pages
    advertising of, 112
    AT&T breakup and, 109–11, 134
    centralizing of publishing operation of, 117
    computer systems of, 116
    marketing innovations of, 119–20
    printing costs of, 115–17
Specialty stores, 6–7, 9–10, 142–44, 148, 150, 159, 163–64. *See also* The Limited; Victoria's Secret
Spot market advertising, 63
Sprite, 41, 43, 45, 52, 61–62
StarLyte, 85, 88, 98, 102, 104
StarSensor, 85
Star Wars (movie), 82, 84, 100
Sunkist, 66
Surf, 41, 43–55. *See also* Slice

Tab, 64
Tastes, changes in, 198
Technology, 90, 93, 97–98, 103–4
    Lazer Tag and, 82–83, 86
    Teddy Ruxpin and, 78–81
    video games and, 79–80
Teddy Ruxpin, 75, 78–82, 90, 94, 105
Teem, 62
Teenagers, 84–85, 101
Television, 124
The Limited, 2, 9, 208
    advertising of, 158–61
    diversification of, 142–43
    fictional collegiate as customer of, 152
    middleman eliminated by, 163–64
    opening of, 142
    prices at, 137
The Limited Express, 143
Tolliver, Lennie-Marie, 129–30

Tortilla chips, 67
Toys. *See* Worlds of Wonder
Tylenol, 177

U.S. News and World Report, 38
U.S. West, 110, 111, 117
Unit Trust Account, 22, 23

Victoria's Secret, 140–41, 146–55,
    157, 160, 208
  customer model for, 152–55
  labels in, 162–63
  The Limited compared to, 164
  sex and, 161–62
  women's fantasies and, 140–41,
    153–54, 161–62
Video games, 79–80
Violence, 99
VISA, 136

Walkman, birth of, 139, 140
Wall Street Journal, 64, 120–23,
    143–44
"Walter Cronkite at Large," 38–39
War toys, 99
Watson, Thomas, 203–4
Wendy's, 7, 189, 196
Wexner, Leslie H., 204–5
  ambition of, 142

Wexner, Leslie H. *(cont.)*
  background of, 141–42, 165
  business sense of, 164
  copying of, 140, 150, 153–54, 156–
    57, 166–67
  instincts of, 139, 143, 160, 164, 167
  photograph collection of, 141, 145,
    146
  traditional marketing techniques
    as viewed by, 137, 139, 155–56
  traveling of, 146, 148–49
White Castle, 176
White Weld, 18
Women, working, 4, 124
Worlds of Wonder, 75–105. *See also*
    Lazer Tag
  advertising and, 78, 100–2
  bankruptcy and, 105
  market research by, 92–97
  social change and, 88–94
  Teddy Ruxpin and, 75, 78–82, 90,
    94, 105
  template of, 77–79, 81, 93, 105

Yellow Pages, 109, 114, 116–17, 119
"You've Got a Friend" (King), 140
Young & Rubicam (Y&R), 17–23, 27,
    33, 39n
Yuppies, 5